Indian
Place Names
in Alabama

By William A. Read

Revised Edition with a Foreword,
Appendix, and Index
by James B. McMillan

The University of Alabama Press

Originally published in 1937 as No. 29
of Louisiana State University Studies

Library of Congress Cataloging in Publication Data

Read, William Alexander, 1869–1962.
   Indian place names in Alabama.

   "Originally published in 1937 as no. 29 of Louisiana
State University studies"—T.p. verso.
   Includes bibliographies and index.
   1. Indians of North America—Alabama—Names.
2. Names, Geographical—Alabama.   I. McMillan, James B.,
1907–   II. Title.
E78.A28R43   1984   917.61′003′21   84-2593
ISBN 0-8173-0230-1
ISBN 0-8173-0231-X (pbk.)

CONTENTS

ACKNOWLEDGMENTS

For necessary help in finding old documents and maps I have repeatedly called on the staff of The University of Alabama Library, particularly Joyce Lamont, Curator of Special Collections, and her assistants, Clark Center, Deborah Nygren, and Gunetta Rich; Sarah Reeves, Documents Librarian; and Frances Barton, Microtext Librarian; and on Alex Sartwell and Dorothy Brady, of the Alabama Geological Survey Library; and on the staffs of the Birmingham Public Library, the Samford University Library, and the Alabama Department of Archives and History. I am grateful for their expertise and patience.

I am also indebted to Kelsie Harder, who suggested several improvements in an early version of the revision, and to I. Willis Russell, Virginia Foscue, and Sandra Sockwell, for helpful criticism.

JAMES B. McMILLAN

November, 1983

FOREWORD

What is the "meaning" of names like *Coosa* and *Tallapoosa*? Who named the *Alabama* and *Tombigbee* and *Tennessee* rivers? How are *Cheaha* and *Conecuh* and *Talladega* pronounced? How did *Opelika* and *Tuscaloosa* get their names? Questions like these, which are asked by laymen as well as by historians, geographers, and students of the English language, can be answered only by study of the origins and history of the Indian names that dot the map of Alabama. These relics, like fossils embedded in rocks, are traces of extinct cultures, of people found by European explorers, infiltrated by traders and settlers, and eventually moved to distant reservations.

Adopted Indian names have two distinct stages of history: (1) as words in a source language, and (2) as names in American English. Ethnolinguists and historians of aboriginal America are interested in the composition of words surviving as place names and in their significance in tribal life. Students of American English onomastics are interested in the date and circumstances of adoption and subsequent alteration and spreading or extinction of the names as English words. Usually there is no relationship between the two stages in the history of a name, except when an Indian name is translated to make an American place name. The name Sylacauga was preserved because its translation 'buzzard's roost' would have been distasteful as the name of a town, but Buzzard's Roost Bluff on the Tombigbee River is a translated name that lasted; the bluff is not a populated place and the name evidently offended no one, may even have seemed picturesque. Names like Black Warrior, Broken Arrow, and Salt Creek would have no rationale if we did not know that they were translated. The etymology of such names clearly contributes to our knowledge of naming processes.

But the widespread curiosity about the meaning of surviving Indian names is harder to understand. We know that *mississippi* meant 'big river' to the Algonquians, but we have no idea what *tennessee* meant to the Cherokees. Both names serve equally well. Whether *alabama* prehistorically had a general meaning

v

like 'brush clearers' or a more specific meaning like 'medicinal herb gatherers' has had no apparent effect on the history of the state. Nevertheless, there is a persistent interest in the etymology of place names of Indian origin, and the "meaning" of such names evidently has symbolic value to many people. To answer the questions of both professionals and laymen about Alabama Indian place names, W. A. Read wrote in 1937 the only extensive study of the subject. His conclusions are careful, informed, and frequently tentative, never dogmatic.

William Alexander Read (1869–1962) was an early leader in the serious study of Southern American English. Trained in Germanic and Romance philology at Göttingen, Heidelburg, Johns Hopkins, Grenoble, and Oxford (where he studied phonetics under Henry Sweet), he wrote extensively on Southern pronunciation and lexical importation. He was a respected member of the American Dialect Society, the Modern Language Association, the Linguistic Society of America, and the English Place Name Society. From 1902 to 1940 he was the head of the English Department at Louisiana State University.

Like a few other philologists of his generation, notably Edward Sapir and Leonard Bloomfield, Read became interested in American Indian languages, studying particularly those spoken in the southeastern states. He made Indian place names one of his special fields and wrote monographs on the names left on the maps of Louisiana, Florida, and Alabama by the aboriginal inhabitants of the region. He was one of the founders of scholarly study of toponymy in the United States, and his *Indian Place-Names in Alabama*, completed in 1936 and published in 1937, is still a primary reference work.

In his review of Read's Alabama book (*American Speech*, 12:212–15), John R. Swanton supplemented the comments on several names and suggested alternative interpretations of a few. In the same journal (13:79–80) Read added ten names and referred to Swanton's review without disagreeing on any point. In the early 1940s I asked him for help in translating Creek names, and he wrote me several times, generously giving me information that I could not find elsewhere. I thus am confident that he would welcome a re-issue of his monograph if he were alive today, particularly one including his own additions and making use of sources that he did not have in 1936.

Not being versed in Muskogee languages, I cannot make the kind of revision that Read would have made. However, having annotated my copy over the years, I have compiled from my notes an appendix which begins on page 85 of this volume, incorporating (1) Read's own additions, (2) Swanton's comments, and (3) information from other post-1936 investigations, especially Virginia Foscue's 1978 study. My sources are listed in the Appendix Bibliography on pages 100–102.

Read's text is reproduced verbatim except for the silent correction of a few obvious typographical errors. The two early maps that he reprinted have been replaced by a map showing the counties and principal rivers of Alabama.

J. B. McM.

Map of Alabama Counties and Principal Rivers

PREFACE

This study deals with the origin and meaning of Indian geographic names in Alabama. It records the pronunciation only of those names on which reasonably trustworthy data could be obtained. It does not include a detailed history either of aboriginal place names in Alabama or of the tribes that formerly inhabited the state. Its primary aim is linguistic; hence it is not concerned with such names as *Colbert* and *McIntosh*, which, though borne by prominent Indians, are manifestly not of Indian origin. Nor does it deal with novel and artificial forms, examples of which are *Abanda, Aladocks, Alaflora, Alaga, Alco, Falco, Flomaton, Florala, Newala,* and *Norala;* or with modern importations from various Indian tongues that were unknown to the Alabama tribes. Some of these imported names are *Chetopa, Cohasset, Cuba, Eutaw, Havana, Idaho, Java, Keego, Kiowa, Klondyke* [sic], *Manila, Manistee, Maricopa, Mattawana, Nenemoosha, Neshota, Nokomis, Nyota* [sic], *Oneonta, Orono,* and fully a dozen more.

During the preparation of this monograph I have drawn freely on the publications of my predecessors in the field, and I have received help from many persons. But as I have long been familiar with a number of Indian dialects, I am obviously unable now to recall every specific instance of my indebtedness. My special thanks I know to be due to Mr. Peter A. Brannon, Curator of the Alabama Department of Archives and History, for generous aid on every phase of my subject; to Dr. John R. Swanton, of the Bureau of American Ethnology, for the analysis of several difficult names; to Professor Roland M. Harper, of the University of Alabama, for timely notes on elusive local pronunciations; to Miss Lila May Chapman, Director of the Birmingham Public Library, for the transcript of an article published many years ago in the Birmingham *Age-Herald;* and finally, to Mrs. L. E. Pirkle, Secretary of the Department of English, Louisiana State University, for assistance in the correction of the proofs of my manuscript.

WILLIAM A. READ

Louisiana State University
September 23, 1936

INTRODUCTION

1. Sources of names.

Almost all the Indian tribes that formerly inhabited what is now the state of Alabama belong to the Muskhogean family. For the present investigation those of the greatest significance are the Choctaw and the Creek or Muskogee; it is, indeed, from the languages of these two that the aboriginal place names of Alabama have in large measure been derived.

The Choctaw at one time occupied Middle and Southern Mississippi, Western Alabama approximately as far as the Bogue Chitto in Dallas County, the southern part of Alabama, the Gulf coast of Western Florida, and a large part of Eastern and Southern Louisiana. Moreover, several small tribes, known as the *Mobile*, the *Naniaba*, and the *Tohome*, who resided in the Mobile region, are classified as members of the Choctaw linguistic group. Such, furthermore, was the importance of Choctaw that it formed the basis of the so-called Mobilian language, or Chickasaw Trade Jargon, which served as a medium of communication for all the tribes of the Lower Mississippi Valley. But the Mobilian language enriched its vocabulary by borrowing words from other Indian dialects than Choctaw. A notable loan to Mobilian is *Mississippi*, which gradually became so popular that it displaced all earlier designations of the river.

The Chickasaw, who inhabited Northern Mississippi, West Tennessee, and the adjacent territory of Alabama, speak nearly the same language as the Choctaw. Divergences between Chickasaw and Choctaw are generally few and slight; here, however, are some illustrations of a perceptible cleavage between the vocabulary of Chickasaw and that of Choctaw:

Chickasaw	*Choctaw*
Big . . . ishto	chit(t)o
Bird . . . foshe, or foshi	hushi
Duck . . . focho	okfochush
Hot, warm . . . pàlle	alohbi *or* làshpa
Long . . . falaha	falaia
Hush, *exc*. . . . sàmanta	issa
Lie, utter a falsehood . . . lushka	holabi
Sugar . . . shokula (from English *sugar*)	hàpi champuli
Woman . . . iho	ohoyo

But Choctaw has borrowed all of these Chickasaw words except *falaha*, *foshi*, *focho*, and *iho*.

Some other small tribes affiliated with the Choctaw—namely, the Chakchiuma, the Houma, and the Pensacola—need not detain us here, whereas the tribal name *Chatot*, which has often been confused with *Choctaw*, seems to have survived in the geographical nomenclature of Alabama.

The towns of the Creek Confederacy, it is now proper to note, once occupied the greater part of Alabama and Georgia, lying chiefly on the Alabama, Coosa, Tallapoosa, Flint, and Chattahoochee, as well as on the numerous tributaries of these five rivers. The Upper Creek towns were situated on the Coosa and Tallapoosa, in Alabama; the Lower Creek towns on the Middle and Lower Chattahoochee River, along the Alabama-Georgia boundary. In the Creek Confederacy various languages were spoken, among which the Yuchi and the Shawnee were the sole representatives of stocks different from the Muskhogean. The Confederacy takes its name from its dominant tribe—the Creek, which is also called the Muskogee.

Hitchiti is the name of a Lower Creek town, which was considered the head of a linguistic group of tribes akin to the Muskogee or Creek. These tribes were the Apalachicola, the Sawokli, the Okmulgee, the Oconee, the Tamali, the Chiaha, and the Mikasuki.

The Upper Creek tribe known as the *Alabama* lived on the Alabama River, just below the junction of the Coosa and Tallapoosa. The name of this tribe has been given to a linguistic group consisting of the Alabama, Koasati, Tawasa, Pawokti, and Muklasa.

As early as 1713 Bienville settled a band of Tensas Indians on the western side of Mobile Bay. The Tensas belong to the Natchez linguistic group of the Muskhogean family.

Before the middle of the eighteenth century a large group of Natchez had left the Chickasaw and joined the Upper Creeks in Alabama.

The Tuskegee, an Upper Creek tribe, spoke a Muskhogean dialect, and the Yamasee were probably related to the Muskhogean linguistic family. A band of the latter certainly lived at one time among the Lower Creeks.

The Apalachee, yet another member of the Muskhogean

family, were driven in 1703 and 1704 from Western Florida by the combined forces of the English and the Creeks under Colonel Moore of South Carolina, and were granted a refuge by the French at Fort Louis de la Mobile, on Mobile River. Bienville had founded this fort in 1702.

The Muskhogean tribes were not the sole Indian occupants of the Alabama territory in the eighteenth century. The Cherokee, a powerful Iroquoian tribe, dominated Northeastern Alabama as well as a vast domain in the Southern Alleghenies.

In the same century, bands of Shawnee, a tribe included in the Central Algonquian family, were settled among the Upper Creeks in Alabama.

The memory of the Yuchi, sole representative of the Uchean stock, is perpetuated by one or two geographic names in Eastern Alabama.

2. Character of names.

The vocabulary of Indian place names is limited in scope, consisting largely of designations of animals, birds, fish, soil, reptiles, water-courses, plants, trees, settlements, and prominent features of the landscape. Some popular elements, for instance, in Choctaw place names are *bok* or *bog*, "creek," *hàcha*, "river," *oka*, "water," *chula*, "fox," *kinta*, "beaver," *sinti*, "snake," *tala*, "palmetto," *tàli*, "rock," and *uski*, "cane." Similar elements abound in place names from other dialects.

Naturally, both personal and tribal names have been conferred on place names, such as *Alabama*, *Chickasaw*, *Choctaw*, *Tuscaloosa*, and *Tuscumbia*.

Most Indian place names are composed of more than one element, and in many dialects a qualifying adjective follows its noun. Hence a term like "black water" would be rendered by Alabama *oki lucha*, Cherokee *ama*—Lower dialect *awa*— *kūŋnagi*, Chickasaw—Choctaw *oka lusa*, Creek *wi(wa) làsti*, and Hitchiti *oki lochi*.

Another significant feature of certain dialects is illustrated by at least two place names in Alabama—Choctaw *Sucarnochee* and Creek *Hachemedega*. The first of these is literally *shukha*, "hog," *i*, "its," *hàcha*, "river"; the second is *hàchi*, "creek," *im*, "its," *àtigi*, "border." This method of indicating expression, which is found also in Chickasaw and Hitchiti, is analogous to the use of the old-fashioned *his*-genitive in English. Thus "John his book," would become in Choctaw "Chan ɪ holisso."

Other important characteristics of the Indian dialects in Alabama will appear in the analysis of the place names. At this point attention may be called to the frequent occurrence of suffixes, diminutive and collective, as well as to various postpositives signifying a place or a site. Illustrations are furnished by names like *Arbacoochee*, *Funacha*, *Opelika*, *Patsaliga*, *Ponkabiah*, and *Wesobulga*.

3. Number and distribution of names.

Some names have doubtless been overlooked in this study; and the list would probably be longer if the United States Geological Surveys, rich as they are in geographic details not recorded elsewhere, were now available for the entire state of Alabama. Unfortunately, not a few counties still lack these surveys.

The number of Indian place names that have survived in Alabama is apparently 231, and the distribution of these names among the dialects is approximately as follows:

Alabama—Tohome	1	Creek	117
Algonquian—Mobilian	1	Hitchiti	7
Algonquian—Shawnee	2	Kasihta	1
Chatot	1	Koasati	1
Cherokee	9	Natchez	1
Cherokee—Mobilian	1	Tawasa	2
Chickasaw	4	Tensas	2
Choctaw	80	Yuchi	1

4. Pseudo-Indian names.

Certain Alabama place names are not derived from any Indian dialect, though some of them may look as if they had been corrupted from Indian sources. Such place names are:

Altoona. A town in Etowah County. This name reproduces *Altoona*, in Pennsylvania, which is in turn identical with *Altona*, in Holstein, Germany, a name signifying "old meadow," from an inflected form like *"auf der alten Au."*

Calumet. A small town in Walker County. *Calumet*, which is sometimes said to be Indian, is a Norman-Picard word for a tobacco pipe.

Chlota. A station on the Louisville and Nashville Railroad in Chilton County. *Chlota* is the first name of a Miss Clark.

Coker. A railroad spur in Franklin County, as well as a village in Tuscaloosa County, bears the name of a Mr. Coker, whereas *Coker* in Monroe County, Tennessee, is a corruption of Cherokee *Kuku,* "squash" (*Cucurbita*) or "pleurisy root" (*Asclepias tuberosa* L.).

Eliska. A hamlet in Monroe County. In the sixteenth century a distinguished rabbi by the name of *Eliska* or *Elisha* was chief of the synagogue of Safed in Upper Galilee. As a personal name the form *Eliska* is not unknown at the present time. As the site of the Alabama village is far from the ancient Creek territory, Creek *iliska,* "gloomy," cannot be considered a possible source of the name.

Hatche. A former railroad station in Hale County. *Hatche* might be taken for a derivative of Choctaw *hàcha,* "river"; in reality it is merely a poor spelling of the family name *Hatch.*

Hightower. A village in Cleburne County. The Alabama *Hightower* is a popular English name, whereas *Hightower,* a place name in Forsyth County, Georgia, and *Hightower,* the name of a creek in Towns County, Georgia, are corruptions of Cherokee *Itawa,* itself a name of uncertain origin.

Kirewakra. This name, in Mobile County, was conferred about 1910 on a citrus nursery managed by a Japanese. *Kirewakra* is of Japanese origin.

Lima. A station on the Central of Georgia Railway, in Covington County. This is not the same as *Lima,* the name of the capital of Peru, but takes its name from a limestone quarry in the neighborhood.

Mexia. A village in Monroe County, named by Mr. Tom Wiggins in 1893 after a town in Limestone County, Texas. The Texas town bears the name of General Thomas Mejia (1815–1867), who gave the land on which the town was built.

Nauvoo. A town in Walker County. This place was named after Nauvoo, an Illinois town which was founded by the Mormons in 1840 and designated by a corruption of Hebrew *Naveh,* "pleasant."

Neenah. A hamlet in Wilcox County. This name is not connected with *Neenah*, in Wisconsin, but was named after a Miss Nina Olinsky.

Odena. A station on the Central of Georgia Railway in Talladega County. *Odena* at once suggests Ojibway *Odena*, "village"; but as a matter of fact this name is based on that of Mr. John P. Oden, who owned a sawmill at this site about eighty years ago.

Onycha. A station on the Louisville & Nashville Railroad, in Covington County. *Onycha* is the Biblical term for an ingredient of the sacred composition that gave a sweet smell when burned.

Tacon. This, the name of a railroad station near Mobile, is not from Choctaw *takon* or *takkon*, "peach," but is that of a former official of the Mobile and Ohio Railroad.

Tekoa. A station on the Manistee & Repton Railway, in Monroe County. The city of Tekoa or Tekoah is mentioned several times in the Old Testament. *Tekoa* is likewise used as a geographic name in Whitman County, Washington.

SYMBOLS AND ABBREVIATIONS

The modern pronunciation of place names is indicated by the use of the International Phonetic Alphabet.

In the transcription of Indian sources the vowels and consonants have, with few exceptions, the value of the equivalent Continental sounds. The following details, however, should be noted:

$\dot{a} = u$ in "cut"
$ai = i$ in "pine"
$ch = ch$ in "chin"
$h+$consonant $=$ German ch in "*auch*"
$j = j$ in "jest"
$\underline{l} =$ voiceless l
$\eta =$ back nasal

Most abbreviations will be readily understood. Perhaps an exception is *BAE*, which stands for *Bureau of American Ethnology*.

INTERNATIONAL PHONETIC ALPHABET

Symbol	Key Word	Transcription	Symbol	Key Word	Transcription
ɑ	cod	[kɑd]	f	fate	[fet]
æ	cad	[kæd]	s	safe	[sef]
ɛ	fed	[fɛd]	θ	thin	[θɪn]
ɪ	kid	[kɪd]	đ	then	[đɛn]
ʌ	cud	[kʌd]	ʋ	vane	[ʋen]
ɔ	caught	[kɔt]	z	zone	[zon]
e	fade	[fed]	l	lane	[len]
i	feed	[fid]	m	main	[men]
u	food	[fud]	n	name	[nem]
o	code	[kod]	p	paid	[ped]
ʊ	could	[kʊd]	t	tame	[tem]
aɪ	wide	[waɪd]	k	code	[kod]
aʊ	loud	[laʊd]	r	rake	[rek]
ɔɪ	coil	[kɔɪl]	w	wake	[wek]
ə	away	[əˈwe]	ŋ	sing	[sɪŋ]
b	bait	[bet]	ʃ	shame	[ʃem]
d	date	[det]	tʃ	chain	[tʃen]
g	gate	[get]	ʒ	rouge	[ruʒ]
h	hate	[het]	dʒ	jail	[dʒel]
j	yoke	[jok]			

ˈ = main stress   ˌ = secondary stress   ː = long vowel

xviii

LIST OF NAMES

A

ABBEVILLE [ˈæbɪvɪl]

A town in Henry County, taking its name from that of a creek in the same county. See the following name.

ABBIE [ˈæbɪ]

A creek in Henry County.
Yattayabba C. La Tourrette, 1844.
Pattayabao Cr. Rand McNally, 1934.
Abbie has been corrupted from an obscure Indian name, for which I can think of no satisfactory translation. I am inclined, however, to regard Hitchiti *yàtipi*, "panther," as a possible source.

Owen suggests that the name, which he writes *Pattayabba*, may be derived from Creek *atàphàlgi*, a compound of atàphà, "dogwood," and *àlgi*, "grove." He renders the Creek term freely by "dogwood."[1]

But if the first element of *Pattayabba* has been transposed from Creek *atàphà*, then the second may be from Creek *àpi*, "trunk of a tree," or "tree."

The old name of the stream is said to have been pronounced [ˌjɑtəˈæbə].

AFFONEE [ˈæfoni; ˈæfəni]

A tributary of Cahaba River in Bibb County.
Afanee C. La Tourrette, 1844.
Afanee Cr. Smith, 1891.
This name is obscure because of its initial vowel. The early spellings seem to point to Choctaw *afana*, "staked" (like a fence).

I am inclined, however, to regard Choctaw *nafoni*, "bones," as the real source. Such a phrase as "on Nafoni Creek" might easily become "on Affonee Creek."

Loss of an initial *n* appears, for example, in *Ahoola Inalchubba*, the name of a tributary of the Tombigbee, as shown on Bernard Romans' map of 1772. In correct Choctaw this name would be *na hollo*, "white man," *im*, "his," and *ahchiba*, "task" —White Man's Task.

[1] *History*, I, 686.

3

ALABAMA [ˌæləˈbæmə]

1. A river about 312 miles long, beginning 11 miles below Wetumpka at the confluence of the Coosa and the Tallapoosa, and joining the Tombigbee 45 miles north of Mobile Bay to form Mobile River.

2. A state, admitted to the Union Dec. 14, 1819.

3. Alabama City, in Etowah County; incorporated Feb. 16, 1891.

4. Alabama Rolling Mill, a station on the Louisville & Nashville Railroad, near Birmingham.

The Alabama Indians, an Upper Creek tribe, were known to the French as early as 1702 as the "Alibamons," and at that time were settled on the upper reaches of the stream which has received their name.

Early French maps usually show this stream as *Rivière des Alibamons*.

Alabama is derived from Choctaw *álba*, "plants," "weeds," plus *ámo*, "to cut," "to trim," "to gather"—that is, "those who clear the land," or "thicket clearers."

There is no foundation in any Indian dialect for the popular translation of *Alabama* by "Here we rest."

ALAMUCHEE [ˌæləˈmʌtʃɪ]

A tributary of Sucarnochee Creek in Sumter County.

Allimucha C. La Tourette, 1844.

Alamucha was an ancient Choctaw town in Kemper County, Mississippi.

This name possibly means "a little hiding place," from Choctaw *alumushi*, a compound of *aluma*, "hiding place," and the suffix *-ushi*, "little." If the second element of the name is Choctaw *asha*, "are there," then the meaning is "hiding places are there."

Simpson Tubby, a well-known Choctaw living near Philadelphia, Miss., thinks that *Alamuchee* refers to a secret Choctaw organization, whose chief formerly resided on Alamuchee Creek. I owe this bit of information to my friend, Mr. Lea Seale.

APALACHEE [ˌæpəˈlætʃɪ]

A stream forming one of the outlets of Tensaw River in Baldwin County.

D'Anville's map, 1732, shows the "Apalaches" at the head of Mobile Bay.

Apalachee, the name of a Muskhogean tribe, is probably from Hitchiti *apalahchi*, "on the other side." Combined with Hitchiti *okli*, "people," it forms the source of the Florida geographic name *Apalachicola*, which refers to people who live on the other side of a stream.

Webster's *New International Dictionary*[2] derives *Apalachee* incorrectly from the Choctaw dialect.

ARBACOOCHEE [ˌɑːbəˈkuɪtʃɪ]

A village in Cleburne County.

Arbacooche. Smith, 1891.

Abihkuchi was an Upper Creek town in Talladega County. The name is Creek for "Little Abihka." The Abihka were an ancient Muskhogean tribe, whose name is of uncertain etymology.

Gatschet translates it by "pile at the base, heap at the root," with reference to the custom of heaping up a pile of scalps at the foot of a war-pole.

According to another view, the Abihka received their name because of the peculiar manner in which they answered questions or expressed approbation. Yet another view is that *Abihka* is a derivative of Choctaw *aiabika*, "unhealthful place."

Delisle, 1718, records the name as *les Abeikas*.

ATOKA [əˈtoɪkə]

A station on the Louisville & Nashville Railroad in Elmore County.

The source of this name is Choctaw *hitoka* or *hotoka*, "ball ground."

Hitoka was likewise popular as the name of one who had become famous as a ball player.

In 1830 a certain Toko was one of the thirty captains in Greenwood Laflore's district of the old Choctaw nation.

About the same time a chief of *Tala*, "palmetto," one of the settlements of the Sixtowns Indians, was named *Toka Hadjo*, "ballground crazy," or "ballground extremely brave."

The Creek term *hadjo*, borrowed by the Choctaw, is an honorable war name.

The Sixtowns Choctaw lived in Newton, Jasper, and Smith Counties, Mississippi.

Atoka, a county in Oklahoma, bears the name of a Choctaw captain.

ATTALLA [ə'tælə, æ-]

A city in Etowah County.

The first settlement here was called *Atale*, which is a corruption of Cherokee *otali*, "mountain."

AUTAUGA [ɔɪ'tɔɪgə]

1. A creek flowing southward into Alabama River in Autauga County.

2. A county established Nov. 30, 1818.

Creek and county perpetuate the memory of an ancient Alabama town situated slightly west of the present Montgomery.

At-tau-gee. Hawkins, *Sketch*, p. 36. 1799.

Atagi. Gatschet, I, 89.

Autauga is said to mean "land of plenty," but the dialects of Alabama apparently furnish no foundation for this analysis. Creek *àtigi*, "border," however, seems to be a reasonably close equivalent of this name.

AUTAUGAVILLE [ɔɪ'tɔɪgəvɪl]

A small town, in the southern part of Autauga County. *Cf.* the preceding name.

B

BACHELE. See GULLETTE'S BLUFF, *infra*.

BASHI ['bæʃaɪ]

1. A creek flowing into the Tombigbee from the east.

2. A village which takes its name from that of the creek; recorded on the Smith map, 1891.

Bashai C. La Tourrette, 1844.

Bashi may be from Choctaw *bachaya*, "line," "row," "course" —hence Line Creek.

It would be tempting to identify Bashi Creek with the one which Bernard Romans records as Basheelawa, in 1772; but Romans' creek lies too far north, and is thought, indeed, to be identical with the present Tickabum Creek in Choctaw County.[2]

[2] Owen, *History*, I, 124.

Nevertheless, *Bashailawaw* may have been responsible for the present spelling of Bashi Creek, according to a plausible suggestion offered me by Mr. Peter A. Brannon.

Bashailawaw means "plenty of sedge grass" or "broom grass," from Choctaw *hàshuk bāsi*, "sedge grass," and *laua*, "abundant."

BEAR SWAMP

A marsh in the southern part of Autauga County, recorded as *Gum Cypress* L. by Smith, 1891. The Choctaw name of this swamp was *kūsha(k)*, "reeds," plus *chipinta*, "little"—Little Reeds. De Crenay, 1733, writes it *Conchapita*.[3]

BIGBEE [ˈbɪgbɪ]

A village in Washington County; recorded in *The Century Atlas*, 1899.

This name is short for *Tombigbee, q.v., infra.*

BIG SWAMP

A tributary of Alabama River in Lowndes County.

Tatum, in *Notes and Observations on the Alabama River*, 1814, calls this stream *Pil-loop, loc. co* or *Big-Swamp Creek*, transcribing Creek *opilofà*, "swamp," by *Pil-loop*, and Creek *ḷàko*, "big," by *loc. co*. The more usual term for "swamp" is Creek *opilwà*.[4]

BLACK BLUFF

A bluff on the west side of the Tombigbee in Sumter County.

Ecor noir. De Crenay, 1733.

Sacktaloosa. Romans, Map, 1772.

The present designation, *Black Bluff*, has come through French *Écore noir* from Choctaw *sakti*, "bluff," and *lusa*, "black."

Romans explains the name, in 1772, by remarking that in this locality there is a kind of coal.[5]

BODKA [ˈbadkə]

A tributary of Noxubee River in Sumter County.

Bodca C. La Tourrette, 1844.

The name seems to have been shortened and corrupted from

---

[3] *Ibid.*, I, 677.
[4] See Hamilton and Owen, *Pub. Ala. Hist. Soc.*, II, 141.
[5] Cited by Hamilton, *Colonial Mobile*[2], p. 281.

Choctaw *hopàtka*, "wide," a plural form used perhaps with reference to the numerous branches of Bodka Creek. See Smith's map, 1891. A literal translation, then, would be "wide creeks," from Choctaw *bok hopàtka*.

Thomas M. Owen translates the name by "wide creek," assuming an archaic or a dialectal singular *pàtka*, "wide," in Choctaw. I do not see any need for this coinage.

BOGUECHITTO [ˌboɪɡ'tʃɪtə; 'boɪɡ'tʃɪtə]

1. A tributary of the Alabama River in Dallas County.

2. A station on the Southern Railroad, formerly the Mobile & Birmingham, in Dallas County.

3. A creek flowing into the Tombigbee in the southwestern part of Pickens County.

La Tourrette's map of 1844 shows Bogue Chitto both as a creek and as a settlement in Dallas County.

Boguechitto signifies "Big Creek," from Choctaw *bok*, "creek," and *chito*, "big."

BOGUE HOMA

A creek in Mobile County, entering Chickasaw Bogue just north of Prichard.

Bogue Hooma. Romans, Map, 1772.

B. Homa or Red C. La Tourrette, 1844.

This name is from Choctaw *bok*, "creek," plus *homma*, "red" —Red Creek.

Red Creek, a stream in the northwestern corner of Washington County, has lost its Indian name.

BOGUELOOSA [boɪɡ'luːsə]

1. A tributary of Okatuppa Creek in Choctaw County.

2. A station on the Alabama, Tennessee & Northern Railroad—of recent application, not being recorded in *The Century Atlas*, 1899.

Bogue Loosa. La Tourrette, 1844.

Bogueloosa signifies "black creek," the source being Choctaw *bok*, "creek," and *lusa*, "black."

The *Bogue Loosa* of Romans' map, 1772, is now called *Taylor's Creek*, in Washington County.[6]

6 Owen, *History*, I, 164.

BOLIGEE [boɪlɪ'dʒiɪ; 'boɪlɪdʒiɪ]

1. A creek in Greene County.
2. A village situated on the creek. The name was first conferred on the stream.

Boligee [village]. Smith, 1891.

This is a puzzling name, for which some possible sources in Choctaw are the following:

baḻichi, "to stab."
baluhchi, "hickory bark" used in the making of arrows.
aboḻichi, "to hit."
apálichi, "a hewer of wood."
apolichi, "to hill corn."
aboḻi, "thicket," plus ushi, "little."

BROKEN ARROW

A creek in Russell County. A Lower Creek town called *Likachka* was situated on the Chattahoochee near this creek.

The source of the name is Creek *ḻi*, "arrows," and *káchki*, "broken," from Creek *káchkitá*, "to be broken." The settlement was evidently founded by Indians who broke reeds there to make arrows, or it received its name because a band of Indians broke away from the Coweta mother town and formed a new settlement.[7]

BUCKATUNNA [ˌbʌkə'tʌnə]

A branch of Buckatunna Creek, Mississippi, crossing the boundary between Wayne County, Miss., and Choctaw County, Ala.

Bacatune. Bellin, 1764.
Bogue-aithee-Tanne. Romans, Map, 1772.

Hamilton translates *Buckatunna* by "creek on the other side," apparently having in mind Choctaw *tánnap*, "the opposite side," or *mishtánnap*, "the other side," as the last element in the name.[8]

I prefer Halbert's translation, "creek at which is the weaving (of baskets)," from Choctaw *bok*, "creek," *a*, "there," and *tána*, "woven."[9]

---

[7] See Owen, *History*, II, 879–880; Swanton, *BAE*, Bul. 73: 229.
[8] *Colonial Mobile²*, p. 284, footnote 3.
[9] *Pub. of the Ala. Hist. Soc., Trans.*, III, 72.

BULGOSA [bʌlˈgoːsə]

A station on the Louisville & Nashville Railroad in Butler County.

My conjecture that *Bulgosa* is merely a distortion of *Bogueloosa* is confirmed by a letter from Mr. Peter A. Brannon. See *Bogueloosa, supra.*

BUTTAHATCHEE [ˌbʌtəˈhætʃɪ]

A river in Marion and Lamar Counties, joining the Tombigbee in Mississippi.

Buttahatchee R. La Tourrette, 1844.

This name is derived from Choctaw *bàti*, "sumac" (*Rhus* L.), and *hàcha*, "river."

BUXIHATCHEE [ˌbʌksɪˈhætʃɪ]

A creek uniting with Waxahatchee Creek in Chilton County.

Buxahatchee Cr. *U. S. Geol. Survey*, Columbiana Quad., 1911.

The first element in this name may be from Creek *pàkacha*, "commander," as has been suggested to me by Dr. Swanton. The second element is Creek *hàchi*, "creek."

C

CAHABA [kəˈhɑːbə]

1. A river in central Alabama, uniting with the Alabama River in Dallas County.

Cabo R. D'Anville, 1732.

Cahawba R. Early, Map of Georgia, 1818.

2. Little Cahaba River, a branch of the Cahaba, in Bibb and Shelby Counties; recorded by La Tourrette, 1844.

3. An old town, now a rural settlement, situated at the mouth of the Cahaba River in Dallas County.

4. A station, spelled *Cahawba*, on the Birmingham, Selma & Mobile Railroad in Bibb County.

5. Cahaba Valley, the region lying between Odenville, St. Clair County, and Montevallo, Shelby County.

Cahaba is derived from Choctaw *oka*, "water," plus *àba*, "above," according to Thos. M. Owen, *History of Alabama*, I, 188.

With *Cahaba* one may compare *Chukkaba*, the name of a

second lieutenant who served under Pushmataha in the Creek War of 1813.[10]

Chukkaba is from Choctaw *chuka*, "house," and *àba*, "above." Another name of this type is *Nanna Hubba*, *infra*.

CAHULGA [kəˈhʌlgə]

A tributary of Tallapoosa River in Cleburne County.

Cahulga Cr. *U. S. Geol. Survey*, Anniston Quad., 1900.

This name probably signifies "canebrake," from Creek *koha*, "cane," and *àlgi*, "grove." But the name may be the equivalent of "cane clan," *àlgi* being used in the sense of "clan" as well as in that of "grove." There was a cane clan among the Creeks.

CALEBEE [kəˈliːbɪ]

1. A tributary of Tallapoosa River in Macon County.

2. A station on the Birmingham & Southeastern Railroad in the same county.

Upper Creek settlements lay on or near Calebee Creek as noted in the following references:

Callobe. Purcell map, about 1770.

Ca-le-be-hat-che. Hawkins, *Sketch*, p. 31. 1799.

Caloebee is also given by Hawkins as the name of the creek.[11]

The origin of this name seems to be Creek *kàlàpi*, "overcup oak" (*Quercus lyrata* Walt.).

CANCHARDEE [kænˈtʃɑːdɪ]

A village situated a few miles northwest of the city of Talladega.

The name signifies "red earth," from Creek *kàn*, "earth," and *chati*, "red."

Kàn for Creek *ikàna* is often found in compound words.

CANDUTCHKEE [kænˈdʌtʃkɪ]

A creek crossing the southern line of Clay County and flowing into Hillabee Creek, in Tallapoosa County.

Candutchkee Cr. La Tourrette, 1844.

The name signifies "boundary creek"—from Creek *ikàna* or *kàn*, "earth," and *tàchki*, "line."

Candutchkee Creek is now known as *Enitachopco*.

[10] *Cf.* Halbert and Ball, *The Creek War*, p. 315.
[11] *Ga. Hist. Soc. Colls.*, IX, 49. *Cf.* Swanton, *BAE*, Bul. 73: 265 ff.

CAPSHAW [ˈkæpʃoː]

A village situated on Limestone Creek in Limestone County.

Old settlers differ with regard to this name, some asserting that it is of Indian origin, others that it is not.

If it is Indian, it is no doubt a corruption of Chickasaw *bok kapàssa*, "cold creek," or *oka kapàssa*, "cold water." The spelling of the name suggests of course an English origin.

CATOMA [kəˈtoːmə]

A creek joining the Alabama River on the northwestern boundary of Montgomery County.

Kit-to-me. Hawkins, *Sketch*, p. 85.

Catoma Cr. La Tourrette, 1844.

The source of this name is Alabama *oki*, "water," and *Tohome*, the name of a Muskhogean tribe whose cabins were situated in 1729 about twenty-two miles above Mobile on the west bank of the Tombigbee River. Note *Tomez*, Delisle's map, 1718.

At one time, however, the Tohome seem to have lived in what is now Montgomery County; for the present *Catoma Creek* is given as *Auke Thomé* on the De Crenay map of 1733. The tribal name cannot be interpreted, a connection with Choctaw *tomi*, "radiant," or "sunshine," being highly uncertain.[12]

CETEAHLUSTEE

A creek just north of Fredonia in Chambers County.

Ceteahlustee C. La Tourrette, 1844.

The source of this name is Creek *sàta*, "persimmon," and *làsti*, "black"—Black Persimmon Creek.

Old residents remember *Ceteahlustee;* but the stream is now called *Veazey Mill Creek*, or *Gaye Creek*.

CHACALOOCHEE [ˌtʃakəˈluːtʃɪ]

An arm of Mobile Bay, about two miles east of the city of Mobile. The name has been changed to *Choccolotta, q. v., infra.*

Chacaloochee Bay. Bache, *Survey*, 1856.

Not a few French names have survived in the Mobile Delta, such as *Bateau Bay, Bayou Minette, Bon Secours Bay, Gasque, Mon Louis Island*.[13]

---

[12] *Miss. Prov. Archives* (1729–1740), page 23, footnote 1; Swanton, *BAE*, Bul. 73: 150 ff.

[13] *Cf.* Hamilton, *Colonial Mobile*[2], p. 514.

Chacaloochee is a semi-French spelling of *shāŋkolushi*, "Little Cypress Tree," from Choctaw *shāŋkolo*, "cypress tree," and *-ushi*, "little."

English reproductions of Choctaw *shāŋkolo* are *Shongaloo*, in Webster Parish, Louisiana; *Shockaloo*, in Scott County, Mississippi; and *Sharcolo* on the old military road in Mississippi.[14]

CHANNAHATCHEE

A tributary of Tallapoosa River in Elmore County. An Upper Creek town called *Atchinahatchi* was situated on this creek.

Channahatchee is composed of Creek *àchinà*, "cedar," and *hàchi*, "creek."

This stream is also known locally as "Cedar Creek"—*cf.* Smith's map, 1891—and the name is not seldom pronounced as if written *Cheney* or *Chinney*.[15]

CHARTEE [ˈtʃaːti]

A tributary of Tallasseehatchee Creek in Talladega County. *Chartee Creek. U. S. Geol. Survey*, Talladega Sheet, 1892.

This name seems to be a corruption of Creek *chati*, "red." There is a great deal of red clay in the vicinity of the stream.

CHATAKHOSPEE

A large creek tributary to Tallapoosa River, Chambers and Tallapoosa Counties.

The local pronunciation is said to be [ˌɪtʃætəˈsɔːfkə].

Gatschet spells the name *Chatoksofke*, with a form nearer to the Indian source than *Chatahospee*, which is preferred by the United States Geographic Board.

The name signifies "Rock Bluff," from Creek *chàto*, "rock," *ak*, "down," and *sufki*, "deep."

Chataksofka was an ancient Upper Creek settlement.

On Smith's map, 1891, this stream appears as *Hoolethlocco Cr. Hoolethlocco* is from Creek *hoḷi*, "war," and *ḷàko*, "big"—Big War Creek. *Holi* is the first element, too, in *Holitaiga*, "War Ford," the name of a Lower Creek town situated in Bartram's time on the Chattahoochee River. Bartram, *Travels*, p. 462, writes it *Hothletega*. Its second element is from Creek *taikità*, "ford."

[14] *Cf. ASP*, Public Lands, VII, 42, ed. G. & S.
[15] See Brannon, *Arrow Points*, VI, No. 1 (Jan. 5, 1923), p. 4.

CHATTAHOOCHEE [ˌtʃætəˈhuɪtʃɪ]

A river forming the lower half of the boundary between Alabama and Georgia.

Chattahochee. Early map, 1818.

This name signifies literally "marked rocks," from Creek *chàto*, "rocks," and *huchi*, "marked."

Pictured rocks are found in the bed of this river.

Hawkins, *Sketch*, p. 52, refers to the "marked or flowered rocks in the river," spelling the name *Chat-toho-che*.

CHATTOOGA [tʃəˈtuːɡə]

A river in Cherokee County and northwest Georgia. The name is also applied to the valley drained by this stream and also to a county in Georgia.

Cherokee *Tsatugi*, usually written *Chattooga*, designated several settlements in the old Cherokee territory. The name may possibly signify "he has crossed the stream," from Cherokee *gatsugi*, "I have crossed"; or "he drank by sips," from Cherokee *gatugia*, "I sip."[16]

CHEAHA [ˈtʃiːhɔː]

1. A mountain on the northern boundary of Clay County.

2. Chehaw, a hamlet northwest of Tuskegee in Macon County; recorded by Smith, 1891.

3. Chehawhaw, or Cheaha, a creek emptying into Choccolocco Creek in Talladega County; recorded by La Tourrette, 1833.

The province of Chiaha, in northern Georgia, was visited by De Soto in 1540.[17]

Settlements of Chiaha Indians existed among the Lower Creeks along the Chattahoochee and Flint Rivers; note, for example, the name *Chiha* on the Mitchell map of 1755.

Chiaha Indians must also have lived farther north in the present Talladega County.

Chiaha may be a derivative of Choctaw *chaha*, "high." The name is not identical with *Cheowa* in North Carolina and *Cheohee* in South Carolina, which are both corruptions of Cherokee *chiyû*, "otter," and *-yi*, "place."

---

[16] See Mooney, *BAE*, Rep. 19, pt. 1: 536.
[17] Bourne, *De Soto*, I, 68; II, 107.

CHEHAW. See CHEAHA, *supra*.

CHEHAWHAW. See CHEAHA, *supra*.

CHEROKEE [ˌtʃɛroˈkiː; *when attributive*, ˈtʃɛroˈkiː]

1. Cherokee Bluff, hills on the Tallapoosa River, above Double Bridge Ferry, in Tallapoosa County.
2. County established Jan. 9, 1836.
3. Cherokee Mills, a station on the Southern Railroad in Cherokee County.
4. A town in Colbert County.

Cherokee, the name of a powerful Iroquoian tribe, is derived from *Tsaragi* of the Eastern Cherokee dialect, to which corresponds the form *Tsalagi* of the Middle and Western dialects. *Tsalagi* is an adaptation of Choctaw *chiluk*, "cave," through the medium of the Mobilian trade language. It is known that some of the Cherokee inhabited caves. *Cherokee* is often pronounced ˈCheroˈkeeː and the medial [o] may become [ə].

CHEWACLA [tʃi-, tʃɪˈwæklə]

1. A creek, tributary to Eufaubee, several miles north of Tuskegee in Macon County.
2. A station on the Central of Georgia Railroad in the same county; recorded in *The Century Atlas*, 1899.

Sawacklahatchee C. La Tourrette, 1844.

Chewacla Cr. Smith, 1891.

The source of this name is Hitchiti *sawi*, "raccoon," *ukli*, "town," and *hàhchi*, "stream."[18]

Sawacklahatchee, infra, is an earlier designation of Chewacla Creek.

Chewacla is not identical with *Chewalla*, the name of a creek in Marshall County, Mississippi. The latter is derived from Choctaw *chuahla*, "cedar."

CHEWALLA [tʃi-, tʃɪˈwɔːlə]

A tributary of the Chattahoochee in Barbour County.

Ho-ith-le-wau-le. Hawkins, *Sketch*, p. 32, 1799.

Clewwallee. Melish, 1814.

Clewalee Cr. La Tourrette, 1833.

Holiwahali was a war town of the Upper Creeks. The name

---

[18] *Cf.* Gatschet, *Cr. Mig.*, I, 144.

signifies "to share out war," from Creek *holi*, "war," and *awa-hali*, "to divide."

This town, in other words, had the privilege of declaring war, and of notifying its allies of an impending conflict. The Rand McNally map of 1934 gives the name as *Clewalia*.

CHICKASANOXIE [ˈtʃɪkəsɔːˈnɑksɪ]

A creek entering the Tallapoosa River at Milltown in Chambers County.

Cohoasanocsa Cr. La Tourrette, 1833.

Konuckse C. S. A. Mitchell, 1835.

Cohoasanocsa Cr. Smith, 1891.

Chickasanoxie Cr. K. H. Gaines, postmaster at Milltown. 1935.

This name was probably first corrupted from Creek *koha*, "cane," and *chanáksi*, "ridge"—Cane Ridge Creek.

La Tourrette's spelling at once suggests a resemblance of the ·first element in the name to the beginning of the Creek term for the cane clan—*Kohasakálgi* or *Kohosálgi*.[19]

But the present form of the name is evidently due to popular confusion of the earlier first element with the tribal name *Chickasaw*. Cf. *Chickasaw, infra*.

CHICKASAW [ˈtʃɪkəsɔː]

A town in Mobile County.

The name is of recent application; not recorded in *The Century Atlas*, 1899.

Chickasaw, the name of an important Muskhogean tribe, with a language closely resembling Choctaw, cannot be translated.

The Choctaw form for Chickasaw is *Chikasha;* the Creek is *Chikasa*.

The Chickasaw pronounce their name *Shikasa* or *Shikasha*.

In *Chickasawhay*, the name of a river in southeast Mississippi, the final element is Choctaw *ahe*, "potato."

CHICKASAW BOGUE [ˈtʃɪkəsɔː ˈboːg]

1. A tributary of the Mobile River in Mobile County.
2. A tributary of the Tombigbee in Marengo County.

Chickasaw Bogue [both streams]. La Tourrette, 1844.

---

[19] Swanton, *BAE*, Rep. 42: 116.

Some modern maps give the name as *Chickasaw Creek* for the stream in Mobile County.

The meaning of *Chickasaw* is unknown, as has just been noted, *supra. Bogue* is Choctaw *bok*, "creek."

CHILATCHEE [tʃɪˈlætʃɪ]

An affluent of Alabama River in Dallas County.

Chilahatchee Cr. Smith, 1891.

This name has been corrupted from Choctaw *chula*, "fox," and *hàcha*, "stream," or "river."

If this were a Creek name, it might be either from *chula hàchi*, "Fox Creek," or from *choli hàchi*, "Pine-tree Creek."

CHILLISADO. See HIGH PINE, *infra.*

CHINNEBY [ˈtʃɪnɪbɪ]

A station on the Louisville and Nashville Railroad in Talladega County.

Chinnibe. Colton, 1855.

Chinnibee. Smith, 1891.

For the name *Chinnaby* see also McKenney and Hall, *History of the Indian Tribes of North America*, II, 194; Swanton, *BAE*, Bul. 73: 284.

Chinnabee was a Creek chief, who was buried on the farm of Mr. Hugh F. McElderry in this neighborhood.

Hawkins, *Sketch*, p. 42, mentions a brother of Chin-a-be, "who has a large stock of hogs, and had ninety fit for market."

The source of *Chinneby* is probably Creek *àchinà*, "cedar," plus *àpi*, "tree."

CHIPOLA [tʃɪˈpoːlə]

A river flowing southward from Houston County, Alabama, through Jackson and Calhoun Counties, Florida.

E. Br. of Chipola R. La Tourrette, 1844.

Chipola bears a formal resemblance to Choctaw *chepulli*, "feast," "great dance," but may be derived more plausibly from Creek *hàchapala*, "on the other side of the stream."[20]

CHISCA [ˈtʃɪskə]

1. A stream on the Southern Railroad in Colbert County.

2. A station on the St. Louis-San Francisco Railroad in Walker County.

[20] *Cf.* the writer's *Florida Place-Names*, p. 46.

Creek *chisca*, "base of a tree," is the source of this name, which must not be confused with Creek *choska*, "post oak" (*Quercus stellata* Wang.). A Lower Creek town by the name of *Chiska talofa*, "base of a tree town," was situated in Henry County, Alabama.

Both these names are of recent application. Nevertheless, several Creek villages were situated on the Tennessee River in northwestern Alabama.

CHOCCOLOCCO [ˌtʃakoˈlako]

1. A large creek in Calhoun and Talladega Counties.
2. A village on the Southern Railroad in Calhoun County.
Chockolocko Cr. La Tourrette, 1833.
Chockolocko or Big Shoal C. La Tourrette, 1844.
Choccolocco [village]. Smith, 1891.
3. Choccolocco Valley lying between Choccolocco Mountains on the northwest and the hills of southeast Talladega County.
4. The Choccolocco Mountains, also called Jacksonville Mountains, forming a high range in Calhoun County.[21]

Choccolocco means "big shoal," from Creek *chahki*, "shoal," and *ĺako*, "big."

CHOCCOLOTTA [ˌtʃakoˈlatə]

This new name for *Chacaloochee Bay*, *supra*, is possibly intended for Choctaw *shäykolo*, "cypress," and *hàta*, "white," White Cypress being an alternative designation of the Bald Cypress (*Taxodium distichum* L.). The second element, however, may be from Choctaw *àtta*, "to stay," "to live."

Yet another possibility is that *Choccolotta* is a derivative of Choctaw *chuka*, "house," or "houses," and *alota*, "big," or "filled."

CHOCTAW [ˈtʃaktɔ]

1. A county established December 29, 1847.
2. A station on the Louisville and Nashville Railroad in Mobile County.

The meaning of *Choctaw*, which in Choctaw is *Chahta*, is unknown.

CHOCTAW BLUFF

A village in Clarke County.

[21] Owen, *History*, II, 805.

CHOCTAW CITY

Post office name *Choctaw*. A village on the Sumter and Choctaw Railroad in Choctaw County.

CHOCTAW CORNER

A community in the northeastern end of Clarke County.

CHOCTAWHATCHEE [ˌtʃɑktɔɪˈhætʃɪ]

1. A river in southeastern Alabama.
2. A creek joining the Choctawhatchee in Dale County.

The first element in *Choctawhatchee* seems to have been confused with *Chatot*, the name of a Muskhogean tribe living near Mobile about 1706; the second element is from Creek *hàchi*, "river," "stream."

Chatot and *Choctaw* (Choctaw *Chahta*) are alike of unknown signification.

CHOLOCCO LITABIXEE

An obsolete Creek designation of Horseshoe Bend, a great curve in the Tallapoosa River in the present Tallapoosa County, famous as the site of a battle in which, on March 27, 1814, General Andrew Jackson's combined American and Indian forces annihilated the Red Stick party of the Creeks, led by Menawa and other chiefs.[22]

Cholocco Litabixee is composed of Creek *choļàko*, "horse's," *ili*, "foot," and *tàpiksi*, "flat"—"Horse's Flat Foot."

Another name given to this site was *Tohopeka*, from Creek *tohopki*, "fort." See *Tohopeka, infra*.

CHUBBEHATCHEE [ˌtʃʌbɪˈhætʃɪ]

A creek flowing southward into Tallapoosa River in Elmore County.

Hatchee Chubbee [creek]. La Tourrette, 1844.

Hatchee Chubbee Cr. Smith, 1891.

Hawkins, *Sketch*, p. 49, translates *Hat-che-chub-bau*, the name of an ancient Creek settlement on this stream, accurately by "middle or halfway creek," deriving it from Creek *hàchi*, "creek," plus *chàbà*, "halfway."

The change of *Hatchee Chubbee* to the present *Chubbehatchee* serves to distinguish this creek from the Hatchechubbee of

[22] Owen, *History*, I, 700–704.

Russell County; but *Hatchechubbee* alone would be strictly correct in the Creek dialect.

CHUCKFEE [ˈtʃʌkfɪ]

A bay flowing from Raft River in Baldwin County.[23]

This name is from Choctaw *chukfi*, "rabbit."

CHULAFINEE [ˌtʃuːləˈfɪnɪ]

1. A creek in Cleburne County.
2. A small settlement on this creek.

Chulafinee Cr. Smith, 1891.

Chulafinee. Smith, 1891.

Chulafinee Creek. *U. S. Geol. Survey*, Anniston Quad., 1900.

This name means "pine log crossing," from Creek *chuli*, "pine," and *fina*, "footlog."

CHUNCHULA [tʃʌnˈtʃuːlə]

A village on the Mobile and Ohio Railroad in Mobile County.

The name is said to have been selected about 1847. It is recorded on the Colton map, 1855.

All attempts to trace this name positively to a Choctaw source will prove to be fruitless. *Chula*, indeed, signifies "fox" in Choctaw, and *chunna* is "lean," "meagre"; but as the adjective follows the noun in Choctaw, this analysis is clearly erroneous.

It is, of course, possible that Choctaw *hachunchuba*, "alligator," together with Choctaw *chula*, may have suggested the coinage of the hybrid form *chunchula*. Owen actually regards *chunchula* as a corruption of Choctaw *hachunchoba* [hachunchuba].[24]

He may be right. But American Spanish contains what is in all probability the source of the name. In various parts of South America a favorite dish is tripe, especially fried lamb tripe; and the Spanish term for this popular food is *chunchullos*, m. pl., or one of its variants—*chunchulli*, m. pl., *chunchúlla*, f. sg., *chunchulas*, f. pl., *chunchules*, m. pl., *chunchulin*, m. sg. (with Spanish diminutive suffix -*in*), *chinchulin*, m. sg., *chinchulines*, m. pl. For the distribution of this term, which in one form or another is found in the dialects of the Argentine Republic,

[23] *Cf.* Hamilton, *Colonial Mobile*², pp. 324, 514.

[24] *Op. cit.*, I, 256.

Chile, Colombia, and Paraguay, one may consult Ciro Bayo, *Vocabulario Criollo-Español Sud-Americano*, p. 82; R. J. Cuervo, *Apuntaciones Criticas Sobre el Lenguaje Bogotano*[6], p. 665; R. Grossmann, *Das Ausländische Sprachgut im Spanischen des Río de la Plata*, p. 8; R. Lenz, *Diccionario Etimológico de las Voces Chilenas Derivadas de Lenguas Americanas*, I, 325–326; and Miguel de Toro, *L'Évolution de la Langue Espagnole en Argentine*, p. 98.

The source of the Spanish term is Kechuan *Ch'unchull*, "tripe."[25]

CHUNNENUGGEE [ˌtʃʌnɪˈnʌgɪ]

A hamlet on the Central of Georgia Railroad in Bullock County.

Chunnenuggee. Colton, 1855.

From Creek *chánánáki*, "long ridge."

CITICO [ˈsɪtɪkoː]

A station on the Tennessee, Alabama & Georgia Railroad in Etowah County. The name is of modern application.

Citico was a Cherokee settlement on Citico Creek, in Monroe County, Tennessee. *Citico*, which is found in Cherokee as *sitiku* or dialectal *sutagu*, cannot be translated.

Citico is the name of a creek and village in Monroe County, Tennessee.

CLAYHATCHEE [kleːˈhætʃɪ]

A village situated in the fork of Claybank Creek and Choctawhatchee River in Dale County.

Clayhatchee owes its name to its location, taking *Clay* from *Claybank* and "*-hatchee*" from Choctawhatchee. *Clay-* refers to the nature of the soil.

Cushman, with his characteristic indifference to sources, derives *Clayhatchee* from Choctaw *chash-ah-huch-cha*, "rattling or rippling river."[26] But the adjective follows the noun in Choctaw; hence "rippling river" would be expressed by *hácha wisákachi*.

The name *Choctawhatchee* is probably due to confusion of the first element with *Chatot; cf. Choctawhatchee, supra*.

[25] E. W. Middendorf, *Wörterbuch des Runa Simi oder der Keshua-Sprache*, p. 398.
[26] *History of the Choctaw, Chickasaw, and Natchez Indians*, p. 605.

COAGIE [ˈkoɪgiɪ]

A creek a few miles southwest of the village of Marble Valley in Coosa County.

Coagie Br. *U. S. Geol. Survey*, Gantts Quad., 1915.

The name probably signifies "cane noise," from Creek *koa* or *koha*, "cane," and *haki*, "noise." As the *g* in *Coagie* is a voiced stop, the second element in the name can hardly be Creek *hàchi*, "stream."

The Choctaw of Bayou Lacomb, Louisiana, are said to call Cane Bayou, in St. Tammany Parish, *chelaha*, "noisy," because of the sound of the wind in the canebrakes along the stream.

COATOPA [ˌkoɪəˈtoɪpə]

1. A creek tributary to the Sucarnochee in Sumter County.
2. A hamlet on the Southern Railroad in Sumter County.

From Choctaw *koi*, "panther," *a*, "there," *hotupa*, "wounded," and [*bok*, "creek"]—Wounded Panther Creek.

COCHGALECHEE

A creek in Russell County. *U. S. Geol. Survey*, Seale Quad., March, 1914.

According to the census of 1832 there was a band of Coweta Indians by the name of *Koochkalecha*.

Gannett translates *Cochecalechee*, the name of a tributary of the Chattahoochee in Georgia, by "Broken Arrow."[27]

In correct Creek "broken arrow" is *ḷi kàchka*, the adjective following the noun *ḷi*, "arrow." *Cochgalechee* or *cochecalechee* means "little broken arrow," though the name has been seriously distorted from Creek *ḷi kàchka uchi* or *ḷikàchkuchi*. There was a Lower Creek town by the name of *Ḷi Kàchka*.

Brannon gives *Cochcalechke* as the name of the creek.[28]

COHABIE

1. A branch of Cedar Creek in Talladega County.
2. A mountain on which Cohabie Creek rises.

Cohabie. *U. S. Geol. Survey*, Gantts Quarry, 1917.

Cohabie possibly signifies "cane stalks," from Creek *koha*, "cane," and *àpi*, "stalks."

The local pronunciation is said to be [kəˈheɪbə].

[27] *U. S. Geol. Survey*, Bul. 258[2]: 86.
[28] *Arrow Points*, Vol. 9, No. 5 (Nov. 5, 1924), pp. 67–68.

COHABADIAH [ko₁habə¹daɪə]

A creek in Cleburne and Randolph Counties.

Cohabadiah Creek. *U. S. Geol. Survey*, Wedowee Quad., 1902.

This name is composed of Creek *koha*, "cane," and *apata-i*, "covering." The name designates an extensive canebrake.

Apata-i is also the source of *Upatoi*, the name of a town in Muscogee County, Georgia, and of *Upatoie*, the name of a creek in the same county.

COLETA [ko¹liːtə]

A small village in the northwest corner of Clay County.

Nothing seems to be known about the origin of *Coleta*, though similar names are found elsewhere. There is a Coleta in Whiteside County, Illinois, as well as a Colita in Polk County, Texas.

Miss Nora Porter selected the name for the Illinois village about seventy years ago, after seeing *Coleta* as the name of a character in a book that she had been reading.

A Koasati settlement by the name of *Colete* lay on the lower Trinity in Polk County, Texas, during the first half of the nineteenth century.

Coleta may be of Spanish origin—some Spanish place names in Alabama of comparatively recent application are *Alameda*, *Andalusia*, *Bermuda*, *Calera*, *Colina*, *Creola*, *Lavaca*, *Palos*, and *Zamora*. If any Spanish place names have survived from the Spanish regime of the eighteenth century, they have escaped my attention.

CONECUH

1. A river of southern Alabama flowing into the Escambia River, in Florida.

Ko-o-ne-cuh. Hawkins, *Sketch*, p. 23.

Ko-ne-cau. Hawkins, *Sketch*, p. 85.

2. A county created Feb. 13, 1818. Its area was subsequently reduced by the creation of Henry, Butler, Covington, and Escambia Counties.

3. A station on the Central of Georgia Railroad in Pike County.

The local pronunciation of *Conecuh* is said to be [kə¹neɪkə].

If *Conecuh* is Creek, it may be a compound of *koha*, "canebrakes," and *ának̇á*, "near." If the name is Choctaw, it may

be from Choctaw *kuni*, "young canes," and *akka*, "below,"
"down there."

Gannett's derivation of the name from Creek *conata* [kunità],
"crooked," is untenable.[29]

So, too, is Cruikshank's translation, "land of cane," from a
hypothetical Creek *Econneka*. In Creek "land of cane" would
be rather *koh*(a), "cane," plus *ikàna*, "land," or *ikàna*, "land,"
in, "its," and *koha*, "cane."

But W. S. Wyman's derivation of the name from Creek *kono
ika*, "pole-cat's head," is by no means improbable.[30]

COOSA [ˈkuːsə]

1. A river formed by the junction of the Oostanaula with the
Etowah at Rome in northwest Georgia. The Coosa, uniting
with the Tallapoosa River eleven miles below Wetumpka, forms
the Alabama River.

Coosee is the spelling of the Melish map, 1814; *Coosa*, that of
the Early map, 1818.

2. A county established Dec. 18, 1832, and named for the
river.

3. A station on the Southern Railway in Fayette County.

4. A station on the Southern Railway in Talladega County.

5. Coosa Valley. A region in Alabama extending from Look-
out Mountains for more than thirty miles towards the west.

On July 16, 1540, the De Soto expedition entered a great
Upper Creek town called *Coça*, which was situated less than
a mile east of Coosa River, in the present Talladega County.

The river took its name from the town.

Coosa is in all probability a derivative of Choctaw *kūsha*,
"cane," "canebrake."

COOSADA [kuˈsɔːdə]

A creek in Elmore County. See *Coosada Station*, *infra*.

COOSADA STATION

A village situated on the Louisville & Nashville Railroad and
on Coosada Creek in Elmore County.

Coosada was founded by colonists from Georgia about 1818,
and takes its name from an Upper Creek branch of the Alabama

---

[29] *Geol. Bulletin*[2], 258: 89.
[30] See Owen, *History*, I, 315, for Cruikshank's and Wyman's translation.

known as the *Koasati*, whose village was situated near the site of the present Coosada Station during the second half of the eighteenth century.

The name may possibly be a derivative of Choctaw *kŭsha*, "cane," and *hàta*, "white"—White Cane.

COPASSAW [ˈkɑpəsɔɪ]

A creek tributary to the Tombigbee River in Choctaw County.

The name is taken from Choctaw *kapàssa*, "cold," which is the second element in the name of a Choctaw village formerly situated on this stream. This village was called *Oka Kapàssa*, "Cold Water."

CORNHOUSE CREEK

A tributary of the Tallapoosa near the village of Malone in Randolph County.

The Okfuski built a settlement in this vicinity which they called *Tohtokagi*, and which Hawkins spells *Tooh-to-cau-gee*.[31]

"Cornhouse" is translated and adapted from a part of the name of the old Indian settlement; for *Tohtokagi* means "standing corncribs," from Creek *tohto*, "corncribs," and *kagi*, "standing," or "set up," a form of *kakità*, "to be," "to sit."

On Smith's map of 1891 the name of the creek appears as *Hoote Archee*. The first element of this term seems to be Creek *huti*, "houses," rather than a corruption of Creek *Tohto;* whereas the second element is evidently intended for Creek *hàchi*, "creek."

COTACO [koˈteɪko]

A creek in Morgan County.

Cotaco C. A. Finley, 1826.

Cotaco seems to be of Cherokee origin; I suggest that it has been abbreviated and corrupted from Cherokee *ikati*, "swamp," or "thicket," and *kunahita*, "long."

Compare the name *Cotocanahut* given in 1755 to an unidentified Cherokee town.[32]

---

[31] *Ga. Hist. Soc. Colls.*, IX, 33.
[32] C. C. Royce, *BAE*, Rep. 5: 142.

COTAHAGA [ˌkoɪtəˈheɪgə]

A tributary of the Tombigbee in the southeastern part of Sumter County.

Cotahager C. La Tourrette, 1844.

Cotahaga Cr. Smith, 1891.

This name may signify the creek "where the locust tree stands," the source being Choctaw *kàti*, "locust tree," *a*, "there," and *hikia*, "standing."

Hikia is used only as a singular; compare *Tallahaga*, the name of a creek in Winston County, Miss., which is derived from Choctaw *tàli*, "rock," and *hikia*, "standing."

The plural of *hikia* is *hieli*, which appears in such names as *Pitchahala*, the designation of a creek in Carroll County, Miss., a compound of Choctaw *pichi*, "sorrel" (*Rumex acetosella* L.), *a*, "there," and *hieli*, "standing"; and *Tallahalla*, a creek in Hinds County, Miss., a derivative of Choctaw *tàli*, "rocks," and *hieli*, "standing."

It will be observed that the first of two successive vowels is often elided in Choctaw, as in *kàt(i)a haga* and *pich(i) a hala*. A similar elision prevails in Creek.

Owen writes the name *Catahager* and derives it from Choctaw *okhàta hikia*, "standing pond or lake."[33] If this translation were correct, some forms of the name would probably have an initial "O"—as, for example, in the case of the Louisiana place name *Catahoula*, which Darby in 1816 and Tanner in 1820 spell *Ocatahoola*. Its source is Choctaw *okhàta*, "lake," and *hullo*, "beloved," or "sacred."[34]

COTTAQUILLA [ˌkatəˈkwɪlə]

1. A creek tributary to Choccolocco Creek in Calhoun County.

2. A mountain in the same county.

Cottaquilla (creek and mountain). *U. S. Geol. Survey*, Anniston Quad., 1900.

The name probably means "dead honey locusts" from Creek *kàtohwa*, "honey locusts" (*Gleditsia* L.), and *ili*, "dead."

Creek *h* before a consonant, as in *katohwa*, sounds like German "ch," as in *auch*, and may be transcribed, though in-

---

[33] *History*, I, 212.
[34] *Cf.* the writer's *Louisiana Place-Names of Indian Origin*, p. 17.

accurately, by *k*. Compare Du Roullet's reproduction, in 1732, of Choctaw *Holahta Tàshka*, "Warrior Chief," by *Oulaka Taska*.[35]

The war title *holahta*, "chief," is found also in Creek, Apalachee, and Timucua.

COWIKEE [kauˈaɪkɪ]

An affluent of the Chattahoochee in Barbour County.

Co-wag-gee. Hawkins, *Sketch*, p. 65.

Cowikee (North Fork, etc.). La Tourrette, 1833.

Hawkins translates this name by "partridge," evidently connecting it with Creek *kowaiki*, "quail"; whereas Hodge, I, 667, gives *kawaiki* as a derivative of Hitchiti *oki*, "water," and *awaiki*, "hauling," "carrying"—Water-carrying [place]. Hodge's translation is preferred.

CUBAHATCHEE [kjuˈbeːhætʃɪ]

1. A creek running into the Tallapoosa between Calebee and Oakfuskee Creeks, in Macon County.

2. A site two miles east of Montgomery.

Kebihatche. Hawkins, *Sketch* (1799), p. 33.

Ke-be-hatchee. Early, 1818.

Cubihatcha. Upper Creek Settlement, Census of 1832, cited, *BAE*, Bul. 73: 437.

Cupiahatchee C. La Tourrette, 1844.

Cupia Hatchee Cr. Smith, 1891.

I suggest as a possible source of this name either Creek *kàpi hàchi*, from *kàpi*, "lye drip," and *hàchi*, "creek"—a creek where lye was made—or Creek *ki-àpi*, "mulberry tree" (*Morus rubra* L.), and *hàchi*, "creek."

There seems to have been a Creek clan named *Kàpichàlgi*, perhaps "Lye Drip Clan."

CULSTIGH

A creek in the northern part of Cherokee County.

Culstia [settlement]. Colton, 1855.

Culstigh Creek. *U. S. Geol. Survey*, Fort Payne Quad., 1900.

I believe *Culstigh* to be a derivative of Cherokee *kulsetsi*, "Honey-locust place," which is in turn an abbreviation of *kulsetsi*, "honey-locust" (*Gleditsia* L.), and *-yi*, "place."

---

[35] *Miss. Prov. Archives*, I (1729–1740), 154.

CUSSETA [kəˈsiːtə]

A small town in Chambers County.

Coseta. La Tourrette, 1844.

Cusseta is synonymous with *Kasihta*, the name of an ancient Lower Creek tribe.

The meaning of *Kasihta* is unknown, though the Creeks themselves connect *Kasihta* with *hasihta*, "coming from the sun."

The Kasihta, indeed, believe that their tribe came from the sun.

CUTTACOCHEE. See VALLEY CREEK, *infra.*

D

DAGUNAHI

At Muscle Shoals on the south side of Tennessee River in northwestern Alabama there were formerly three Cherokee villages. In 1798 the most important of the three was situated near the mouth of Town Creek.

The Cherokee called Muscle Shoals *Dagunahi*, "mussel place," from *daguna*, "mussel," and *-hi*, "place."

Another name that they used was *Chustanalūyi*, "Shoals Place," a plural formation from *Ustanali*, which is shortened in turn from *Ustanalahi*, "Place of rocks across a stream." From *Ustanali* has likewise come *Oostanaula*, the name of a river in Georgia, as well as *Eastanollee* and *Eastaunala*, names of Creeks in Tennessee.

DOLIVE. See TAWASHA, *infra.*

E

EAST TALLASSEE [ˈiːst ˈtæləsɪ]

A town situated on the east bank of the Tallapoosa River in Tallapoosa County.

Old Tal-e-see. Hawkins, *Sketch* (1799), p. 39.

An Upper Creek town, known as *Talase* or *Big Talasse*, was situated on the east bank of the Tallapoosa in the northwest corner of Macon County. This was the site of the settlement marked *Talisi* on the La Tourrette map of 1833, whereas the present East Tallassee corresponds to La Tourrette's *Tallassee*

(1844), shown several miles farther north on the east bank of the river.

Tallassee is usually thought to be a compound of Creek *tàlwa*, "town," and *hasi*, "old," but this analysis is not absolutely sure. Hawkins, *Ga. Hist. Soc. Colls.*, III, 26, derives *Tal-e-see* from forms equivalent to Creek *tàlofa*, "town," and *isi*, "taken"—that is, "captured town."

Tallahassee [ˌtælǝˈhæsɪ], the name of a city in Florida, is clearly derived from Creek *tàlwa*, "town," and *hasi*, "old"— Old Town.

EGONIAGA [ɛˌgoːniˈeːgǝ]

A tributary of Choccolocco Creek in Calhoun County.

Egoniaga Creek. *U. S. Geol. Survey*, Anniston Quad., 1900.

This name is possibly a derivative of Creek *ikàna*, "earth," and *hauki*, "hole"—that is to say, "cave."

ELKAHATCHEE [ˌɛlkǝˈhætʃɪ]

A creek in Coosa and Tallapoosa Counties.

Alkehatchee. De Brahm, eighteenth century MS., quoted by Gatschet, *Cr. Mig.*, II, 182.

Elkehatchee [cr.]. La Tourrette, 1833.

Alkehatchee was an Upper Creek village in Tallapoosa County.

Elkahatchee may possibly be derived from Creek *ahalak hàchi*, "potato creek," or be abbreviated from *Ahalagàlgi hàchi*, "potato clan creek."

ELM BLUFF

A bluff on Alabama River a few miles south of Cedar Creek in Dallas County.

Elm Bluff. Smith, 1891.

On the De Crenay map of 1733 this bluff appears as *Chacteouma*, a name derived from Choctaw *sakti*, "bluff," and *homma*, "red"—Red Bluff.

ELWA

A creek tributary to Fowl River in the southern part of Mobile County.

Data on this name are lacking. If it is Indian, it may be a corruption of Choctaw *hàlwa*, "soft-shelled turtle."

EMAUHEE

A creek tributary to Tallasseehatchee Creek about a mile below the town of Sycamore in Talladega County.

Emauhee C. La Tourrette, 1844.

Emauhee may be a man's name, perhaps Creek *immahi*, "father-in-law." Another possibility is that the name has been corrupted from the Creek title *imała*, "leader." The form *Emarhe* (1836) designates a former Creek town on Apalachicola River, which was also known as "Ematlochee's town."

Ematlochee is derived from Creek *imała*, "leader," plus the diminutive suffix *-ochi*, "little."

The voiceless *l* of *imała* might have developed a *u*-glide and then disappeared itself, *imała* becoming *imaua* or *imauha*, whence the present Emauhee.[36]

EMUCKFAW

A tributary of Tallapoosa River about fifteen miles east of Alexander City, Tallapoosa County.

Hawkins, *Sketch*, p. 46, writes *Immookfau* and interprets the name by "gorget made of a conch."

Hitchiti *imukfa* signifies a shell or a concave metallic ornament.

ENITACHOPCO [iːˌnɪtəˈtʃɑpko]

A large creek formerly called *Candutchkee*, in Clay County.

An ancient Hilibi village, which Hawkins, *Sketch*, p. 43, calls *Au-net-te Chap-co*, was situated near this stream.

The name is from Creek *anàti*, "thicket," and *chàpko*, "long" —Long Thicket Creek.

ESCAMBIA [ɛsˈkæmbiə]

1. A river in south Alabama and northwest Florida, emptying into Escambia Bay, Florida. A branch of this river in Escambia County is called *Escambia Creek*.

2. A county named in 1868 for the river, which flows through the county.

Escambia R.; Little Escambia R.   Early, Map of Georgia, 1818.

In a review of the writer's *Florida Place-Names of Indian*

---

[36] See Hodge, I, 422; Swanton, *BAE*, Bul. 73: 284, 437.

Origin, Dr. John R. Swanton suggests Choctaw *uski,* "cane," and *àmo,* "to gather," as the source of *Escambia.*[37]

Owen proposes Choctaw *oski,* "cane," and *ambeha,* "therein," taking *ambeha* for a rare form of *abeha,* "to be in."[38]

ESCATAWPA [ˌɛskəˈtɔːpə]

1. A river in southwest Alabama, flowing through southeast Mississippi and emptying into Pascagoula River in Jackson County, Miss.

2. A town on the Mobile & Ohio Railroad in Washington County.

Escatawpa C. La Tourrette, 1844.

This name signifies the creek where cane was cut, from Choctaw *uski,* "cane," *a,* "there," and *tápa,* "cut."

ESTABOGA [ˌiːstəˈboːɡə]

1. A town on a creek of the same name in Talladega County. This was a former Upper Creek settlement.

2. A creek tributary to Choccolocco Creek.

This name means "people's dwelling place," from Creek *isti,* "people," and *àpoga,* "dwelling place" < *àpokita,* "to dwell."

ETOWAH [ˈɛtowaː]

1. A county established Dec. 1, 1868.

2. A station on the Mobile & Gulf Railroad in Tuscaloosa County.

The county was named after the Etowah mound in Georgia.

Itawa was the name of at least two Cherokee settlements, the one on Etowah River, in Forsyth County, Georgia, the other in Towns County, Georgia. *Itawa* has survived in *Etowah,* the name of a river in Georgia, and has been corrupted to *Hightower* and *High Tower,* both place names in Georgia.

The name of a large village called *Itaba, Ytaua,* or *Ytava* in the chronicles of De Soto, 1540, is possibly of the same origin as Cherokee *itawa.* If so, *itawa* may perhaps be connected with Creek *itàlwa,* "town," "tribe."

EUFAULA [juˈfɔːlə]

A city on the west bank of the Chattahoochee in Barbour County.

[37] *American Speech,* IX, No. 3 (October, 1934), 219.
[38] *History,* I, 548–549.

The founding of the city goes back to 1833.

Eufaula designated a number of Creek settlements, one of which was situated near the site of the present city.

Eufaula cannot be translated.

EUPHAUBEE [juˈfɔɪbɪ]

An eastern tributary of Tallapoosa River in Macon County.

Eu-fau-be. Hawkins, *Sketch* (1799), p. 26.

Eufaubee Creek. Owen, *History*, II, 919.

The signification of *Eufaubee* is unknown. But I surmise that it is merely a variant of *Naufaba*, *infra*, with the loss of an earlier *n-* after the manner of words like *adder*, *apron*, and *auger*. *Naufaba* derives from Hitchiti *nofāpi*, a compound of *nofi*, "beech," and *āpi*, "tree."[39]

F

FAKITCHIPUNTA

A creek in Choctaw County now called *Turkey Creek*.

An old Choctaw stockade, which took the name *Fakitchipunta* from that of the creek, was situated on the Tombigbee River, partly in Choctaw and partly in Clarke County. The Americans knew this settlement as "Tombigbee Turkey Town."

Fakitchipunta is Choctaw for "Little Turkeys," its source being *fakit*, "turkeys," and *chipunta*, "little."

FALAKTO [fəˈlæktoɪ]

A station on the Louisville & Nashville Railroad in Chilton County. The name is of comparatively recent application.

Choctaw *falakto* means "fork" or "forked," as in *bok falakto*, "the fork of a creek," or "a forked creek."

FINIKOCHIKA [ˌfɪnɪˈkɑskɪ]

A creek just west of Weogufka Creek in Coosa County.

Finikachika Creek. *U. S. Geol. Survey*, Gantts Quarry, 1917.

This name means "Broken Foot-log" Creek, from Creek *finà*, "foot-log," and *kàchki*, "broken."

FIXICO [ˈfɪksɪko]

A creek in Randolph County. *U. S. Geol. Survey*, Wedowee Quad., 1902.

[39] Gatschet, *Cr. Mig.*, II, 111.

Fiksiko, "heartless," is a popular element in Creek war names, as in *Icho fiksiko,* "Deer fiksiko," *Nokos fiksiko,* "Bear fiksiko," *Osàna fiksiko,* "Otter fiksiko."

FOSHEE [ˈfɑʃɪ]

1. A village in Escambia County.
2. A station on the Mobile & Ohio Railroad in Montgomery County.

This name, of comparatively recent application, is a derivative of Chickasaw *foshi,* "bird."

In the Alabama and Hitchiti dialects "bird" is *fosi;* in Choctaw it is *hushi.*

The hybrid of *Fosheeton—Foshee* and *-ton,* "town"—which is recorded by Smith, 1891, and *The Century Atlas,* 1899, has disappeared from recent maps. Fosheeton, a rural community, is situated in Tallapoosa County, northeast of the present Alexander City.

FUSIHATCHI [ˌfʌsɪˈhætʃɪ]

A creek entering the Tallapoosa River near the hamlet of Ware in Elmore County.

Fus-hatchee was an Upper Creek settlement, which Hawkins calls *Foosce-hot-che.*[40]

The source of this name is Creek *fuswa,* "bird," and *hàchi,* "stream."

G

GAYE CREEK. Cf. CETEAHLUSTEE, *supra.*

GULLETTE'S BLUFF

An elevation on the east bank of Alabama River below the mouth of Pursley Creek in Wilcox County; shown on Smith's map, 1891.

The Choctaw name for this bluff was *bàhcha illi,* "Dead Ridge," from *bàhcha,* "ridge," and *illi,* "dead."

On the De Crenay map of 1733 the name is spelled *Bachelé.*

GUNTERSVILLE

The county seat of Marshall County.

The Cherokee founded a town in 1790 at the present site of

[40] *Ga. Hist. Soc. Colls.,* IX, 168.

Guntersville, and named it *Kusa-Nūnahi*, "Creek Trail," from Cherokee *kusa*, "Creek Indian," and *nūnahi*, "path."

The Creek Path was an old trail from South Carolina, passing through what is now Rome, Georgia, and reaching the Tennessee River at the present site of Guntersville. The traders knew the Indian settlement as *Creek Path;* but it received several other names before it was finally called *Guntersville*, in August, 1848, after John Gunter, an early settler who married a Cherokee.

H

HACHEMEDEGA [ˌhætʃməˈdiːɡə]

A creek south of Rockford in Coosa County.

Hachemedega Cr. *U. S. Geol. Survey*, Wetumka Quad., 1903.

This name signifies "Border Creek," from Creek *hàchi*, "creek," *im*, "its," and *àtigi*, "border." *Hachemedega* refers to a creek situated on a boundary line. *Cf.* the meaning of *Talladega*, *infra*.

HALAWAKEE [ˌhæləˈwækɪ]

1. A tributary of the Chattahoochee in Lee County.
2. A station on the Chattahoochee Valley Railroad in Lee County.

Hollowockee. Hawkins, in *Georgia Hist. Soc. Colls.*, IX, 61, Jan. 20, 1797.

Halawaka Cr. Smith, 1891.

Halawaka [village]. Smith, 1891.

Creek *holwaki*, "bad," is the source of this name.

HATCHECHUBBEE [ˌhætʃɪˈtʃʌbɪ]

1. A creek in Russell County.
2. A town on the Central of Georgia Railroad in the same county.

Hat-che chub-bau. Hawkins, *Sketch*, p. 49.

Hatcheechubbee [cr.]. La Tourrette, 1833.

A Lower Creek village was situated near the present town of Hatchechubbee.

This name is derived from Creek *hàchi*, "creek," and *chàbà*, "halfway"—Halfway Creek. *Cf. Chubbehatchee*, in Elmore County, *supra*.

HATCHET CREEK

1. An eastern affluent of Coosa River in Coosa County.
2. A village in Clay County.

Po-chuse-hat-che. Hawkins, *Sketch*, p. 50, 1799.

Hatchet C. La Tourrette, 1833.

An Upper Creek town by the name of *Pochushatchee* was situated on Hatchet Creek in what is now Clay County.

Creek *Pochushàchi* is syncopated either from *pochuswuchi hàchi*, "hatchet creek," or from *pochuswa hàchi*, "ax creek." The Indian name of this stream is no longer used.

HATCHETIGBEE [ˌhætʃɪˈtɪgbɪ]

A bluff on the Tombigbee about two miles and a quarter below Santa Bogue Creek in Washington County.

Atchatickpé, "a large bay or lagoon." Romans, Map, 1772.

Hatchetigbee Bl. Smith, 1891.

Hamilton[41] observes that Romans' bay or lagoon was filled and cultivated long ago. *Hatchetigbee*, however, does not mean "Neck of Bottle Stream," as Hamilton suggests, but derives from Choctaw *hàcha tikpi*, "river knob."

HAYSOP [ˈheɪsɑp]

A tributary of Cahaba River in Bibb County.

Haysoppy. La Tourrette, 1844.

If the name of this creek is of Indian origin, it may be a corruption of Choctaw *hush àpa*, "the black gum" (*Nyssa* L.). The Choctaw gave this name to the tree because birds (*hushi*) like to eat (*àpa*) its berries.

Other derivations that occur to me are Choctaw *ahe*, "potatoes," plus *sipi*, "old," and Choctaw *ahe*, "potato," plus *osapa*, "field."

HIAGGEE

A tributary of the Chattahoochee near the town of Oswichee in Russell County.

Ihagee Cr. Smith, 1891.

Ihagi or *Haihagi*, the name of a former Lower Creek town in this neighborhood, signifies "the groaners," from Creek *haihkita*, "to groan."

Hiaggee is said to be the local form.

[41] *Colonial Mobile*[2], p. 284, footnote 2.

HIGH PINE

A creek crossing the southern line of Randolph County and joining Tallapoosa River near Abanda in Chambers County.

La Tourrette, 1844, and Smith, 1891, record *Chillisado* for the name of this stream. *Chillisado* is corrupted from Creek *choli*, "pine tree," and *satahi*, "trimmed." The Creek for "High Pine" would be *choli chapko;* but if the name refers to a stream situated in a high piny region, the Creek term would be *choli*, "pine," plus *halwi*, "high." The Indian name is no longer used.

HILLABEE [ˈhɪləbɪ]

1. A creek in Clay and Tallapoosa Counties, formed by the junction of Little Hillabee and Enitachopco Creek.
2. Hillabee Ridge, a range of hills and mountains in Tallapoosa County.

Hilibi, the name of an ancient Upper Creek town situated near the creek, is derived from Creek *hilapki* or *hilikbi*, "quick."

HOOLETHLOCCO. See CHATAKHOSPEE, *supra.*

HOOTE ARCHEE. See CORNHOUSE CREEK, *supra.*

HORSESHOE BEND. See CHOLOCCO LITABIXEE, *supra.*

HOSPILIKA [ˌhɑspɪˈlaɪkə]

A creek in Lee County.

Hospilika Creek. *U. S. Geol. Survey*, Opelika Quad., 1909.

Hosapoligee. Gatschet, *Cr. Mig. Legend*, II (1888), 65.

This name refers to a stream on the banks of which there are, or were, yaupon trees. *Hospilika* is composed of Creek *asi*, "yaupon," *api*, "trees," and *laiki*, "place." Compare the derivation of *Ocelichee, infra.*

HUXAGULBEE

A tributary of the Coosa River just north of Weogufka Creek in Coosa County.

Huxagulvee C. La Tourrette, 1844.

Huxagulbee Creek. Brannon, *Hdb.*, 1920, p. 53.

I can suggest no satisfactory analysis of this name. It may have been corrupted from Creek *ochi*, "hickory," and *kalpi*, "dry."

I

ILLKINASK

A tributary of the Tombigbee west of Coffeeville in Clarke County.

The name of this creek is shortened and corrupted from Choctaw *Iŋkilish*, "English," and *Tàmaha*, "town."

Inkillis [Iŋkilish] Tàmaha was one of the original Sixtowns people.

K

KAHATCHEE [ˈkəˈhætʃɪ]

1. A creek tributary to Coosa River in Talladega County.

2. A group of mountains, locally called *Kahatchie Hills* in the same county.

Both creek and mountains are shown on the *U. S. Geol. Survey*, Gantts Quadrangle, 1917.

An Upper Creek town called *Cohatchie* was situated in southwest Talladega County.

Kahatchie is contracted from Creek *koha*, "cane," and *hàchi*, "creek."

KANETUCK

A small stream about four miles east of Irondale in Jefferson County.

Kanetuck Branch. *U. S. Geol. Survey*, Leeds Quad., 1907.

I am inclined to take *Kanetuck* for a corruption of Choctaw or Chickasaw *kantak*, "smilax," a plant from the roots of which the Choctaw made bread.

In the *American State Papers*, series of public lands, VII (ed. Gales & Seaton), pp. 116, 138, there is a reference to a Choctaw Indian by the name of *Kentuck John*.

Kentuck may be a corruption either of Choctaw-Chickasaw *kantak* or of *kinta*, "beaver," plus *oka*, "water."

Perhaps *Kanetuck*, too, may signify either "smilax" or "beaver water."

Kantak pàska is Choctaw for "kantak bread."

KATALA [kəˈtælə]

Mountains lying north of Fayetteville and east of Coosa River in Talladega County.

Katala Mountains. *U. S. Geol. Survey*, Talladega Sheet, 1892.

Katala seems to be composed of Creek *ki*, "mulberry" (*Morus rubra* L.), or "mulberries," and *tali*, "dead." Such is clearly the meaning of *Ketale*, the name of a stream on which Hawkins, *Sketch*, p. 55, found several Coweta settlements, and which as early as 1835 became known as "Mulberry Creek," in the present Harris County, Georgia.

KENTUCK

A mountain in the northeastern part of Talladega County.
Kentuck Mountain. *U. S. Geol. Survey*, Anniston Quad., 1900.

The source of *Kentuck* is possibly Creek *kintàki*, "dwarfish," "scrubby." But as *Kentuck* is apparently not an old name, it may be a popular abbreviation of *Kentucky*. *Kentucky* is of uncertain etymology; it may contain Iroquois *kenta*, "prairie."

KETCHEPEDRAKEE [ˌkɛtʃɪpəˈdreɪkɪ]

A creek joining the Tallapoosa River in the northern part of Randolph County.
Ketchepedrakee C. La Tourrette, 1844.

The source of this name is Creek *kicho*, "mortar," and *pàtaki*, "spread out," the designation of a block of wood used in the pounding of Indian corn.

KEWAHATCHIE

A village on the Louisville & Nashville Railroad in Shelby County.
Kewahatchie. U. S. Geol. Survey, Columbiana Quad., 1911.

The name is thought to be that of an Indian who lived at the present site of the village.

The first element in this name is not clear to me; it is suggestive, however, of Creek *ki*, "mulberry." The second is probably Creek *hàchi*, "creek."

KILLYCASIDDA

A small branch tributary to Town Creek in Colbert County: recorded on the *U. S. Geol. Survey*, Rogersville Quad., 1914.

This name is apparently derived from Chickasaw *kàli*, "spring of water," and *oka sita*, "water edge"—that is, the border or edge of a spring.

Mr. F. W. McCormack, of Leighton, Alabama, gives me the local pronunciation of this name as [ˌkɪtɪˈkæskiə], which points to a compound of Chickasaw *kàti*, "honey locust," and *kushkoa*, "bent and broken." I am strongly inclined to regard the latter form as the original Indian term.

KINSACKS CREEK

A tributary of the Tombigbee from the east, just north of Coal Fire Creek in Pickens County.

This name, which is recorded by La Tourrette, 1844, seems to be a corruption of Choctaw *kūshak*, "cane," "reed."

KINTERBISH [ˈkɪntəbɪʃ]

A creek in Sumter and Choctaw Counties.

Kintabish C. La Tourrette, 1844.

From Choctaw *kinta*, "beaver," and *ibish*, "lodge."

For a similar use of *ibish*, compare Choctaw *ahe ibish*, "potato hill," and *peni ibish*, "the bow of a boat," or "the stern of a boat."

KOWALIGI

1. A village in Elmore County.
2. A creek called now *Little Kowaligi* in the same county.

Kowaligi is corrupted from Creek *ika*, "his head," and *ilàidshas*, "I kill." *Cf. Kialijah C.* La Tourrette, 1844.

KULUMI

An ancient Upper Creek town situated on the Tallapoosa River, at first on the north bank in the present Elmore County, but subsequently on the south bank in Montgomery County. Indian mounds distinguish the latter site.

Kulumi is probably derived from Creek *kàlà*, "white oaks," and *omin*, "where there are."

KŪSHA(K) CHIPINTA. See BEAR SWAMP, *supra*.

KUSHLA [ˈkuʃlə]

A hamlet in Mobile County, named about 1847; recorded by Colton, 1855.

Kushla is considered locally to be of Indian origin. If it is Indian, it may be from Choctaw *kūsha*, "reeds," "canes," and *hieli*, "standing." Or it may possibly be from Choctaw *akushli*, "bent down," the past participle of *akochofa*, a term used with reference to the practice of bending down cornstalks to protect the ears from the weather or birds.

KYMULGA [kaɪˈmʌlgə]

A village on the Southern Railroad in Talladega County. The name has also been given to a cave in this neighborhood.

About the middle of the eighteenth century there was a Shawnee town known as *Cayomulgi, Kiamulga,* or *Kiomulgee,* situated east of Coosa River at or near the present Kymulga.

La Tourrette's map of 1833 shows a "Kiomulkee Road" slightly north of the site of Kymulga.

Kymulga is derived from Creek *ki,* "mulberries," and *omálgà,* "all."

L

LADIGA [ləˈdaɪgə]

A station on the Southern Railroad in Calhoun County.

Ladiga.   Colton, 1855; *U. S. Geol. Survey,* Anniston Quad., 1900.

This name is said to have been that of a Creek chief, whose picture is given in McKenney and Hall's *Indian Tribes of North America,* Vol. III, facing p. 72.

In this volume the chief's name is written *Ledagie.*

Ledagie may possibly be a corruption of Creek *litkà,* "runner," or of Creek *litaikità,* "to have run."

LETOHATCHEE [ˌliːtoˈhætʃɪ]

A town situated in Lowndes County about a mile north of Big Swamp Creek—a stream which Major Howell Tatum referred to in 1814 as *Pil-loop,* or *Big Swamp,* and also as *Letohatchie.*

Letohatchee Creek is a tributary of Alabama River.

The town, which was founded between 1850 and 1860, takes its name from that of the creek.[42]

Letohatchee is derived from Creek *ḷi,* "arrow," *ito,* "wood," and *hàchi,* "stream."

I do not think that the name has been corrupted from *Litafatchi,* the name of an ancient Upper Creek town which was situated in St. Clair County, Alabama.

Gatschet associates *Litafachi* with the making of arrows. I analyze it as a compound of Creek *ḷi,* "arrow," *ito,* "wood," and *fàchità,* "to straighten"—that is, "those who make arrows

---

[42] Owen, *History,* II, 876.

straight." But the last element may be Creek *fàchi*, "right," "straight."

The name is also written *Littefutchi*.

Major Tatum's *Pil-loop* is a corruption of Creek *Piḷḷàko*, which is composed in turn of *opilwa*, "swamp," and *ḷàko*, "big."

LIKACHKA. See BROKEN ARROW, *supra*.

LINE CREEK. See OAKFUSKEE, *infra*.

LITTLE CHATAHOSPEE

A branch of Chatahospee Creek in Chambers County. The United States Geographic Board rejects the name *Little Hoolethlocco*. See *Chatahospee, supra*.

LITTLE HILLABEE

A creek in Clay County. See *Hillabee, supra*.

LITTLE LOBLOCKEE CREEK

This stream is situated on the boundary between Chambers and Lee Counties. See *U. S. Geol. Survey*, Opelika Quad., 1903–1907.

Loblockee signifies "big cane," a corruption of Creek *ḷawa*, "cane," and *ḷàko*, "big"—hence "Little Big Cane Creek." In 1832 an Upper Creek town was called *Laplàko*.

Gatschet, *Cr. Mig. Leg.*, I, 137, gives the equivalent of Creek *ḷap* as the name of cane of which the blowguns were made.

The Fifth Report of the United States Geographic Board, p. 196, omits "little" from the name of the creek.

LITTLE OAKMULGEE

A creek. See OAKMULGEE, *infra*.

LITTLE PATSALIGA CREEK. See PATSALIGA, *infra*.

LITTLE TALLAPOOSA. See TALLAPOOSA, *infra*.

LITTLE UCHEE. See UCHEE, *infra*.

LOACHAPOKA [ˌloːtʃəˈpoːkə]

A village in Lee County.

An Upper Creek town by the name of *Lutchapoga* was situated on the Tallapoosa River in Randolph County.

This name is derived from Creek *locha*, "turtle," and *poga*, "killing place"—freely "Turtle Resort."

LOCK

A station, not of Indian origin, on the Seaboard Air Line in St. Clair County.

An Upper Creek town by the name of *Otipalin* was situated at or near the site of Lock. *Otipalin* signifies "Ten Islands," from Creek *oti*, "islands," and *palin*, "ten."

LOCKCHELOOGE [ˌlɑktʃɪˈluːdʒɪ]

A creek in Cleburne County.

Lockchelooge Creek. *U. S. Geol. Survey*, Anniston Quad., 1900.

The first element in this name is Creek *lokcha*, "acorn"; the second is possibly Creek *lachi*, "branches," or Creek *holochi*, "bright," "glistening."

The second element, however, may be Creek *ļako;* for the *dʒ*-sound in the last syllable of the modern pronunciation of the word may be due to the influence of the spelling.

LUBBUB [ˈlʌbʌb]

A tributary of the Tombigbee in Pickens County.

Lubbub C. La Tourrette, 1844.

From Choctaw *lahba*, "warm." The full name would probably be *oka lahba*, "warm water," or *bok lahba*, "warm creek."

LUXAPALLILA [ˌlʌksəpəˈlaɪlə]

A creek flowing through Fayette and Lamar Counties, Alabama, and uniting with the Tombigbee several miles below Columbus, Miss.

Luxapallila or Floating Turtle Cr. Smith, 1891.

The name is derived from Choctaw *luksi*, "turtle," *a*, "there," *balàli*, "crawls," and [*bok*, "creek"].

M

MAUVILLA [mɔɪˈvɪlə]

A village in Mobile County.

Mauvilla. Colton, 1855.

This name resembles some of the early Spanish forms for Mobile. *Cf. Mobile, infra.*

MISSISSIPPI SOUND [ˌmɪsɪˈsɪpɪˈsaʊnd]

That part of the Gulf of Mexico which lies off the coast of Mississippi and Mobile County, Alabama.

Mississippi signifies "big river," its ultimate source being Algonquian *misi*, "big," and *sipi*, "river."[43]

The popularity of this Algonquian name was largely due to its adoption by the Mobilian trade language.

The Chickasaw applied the term *sakti ḷáfa*, "furrowed bank," or "ridged bluff," to the Chickasaw Bluff on the Mississippi at Memphis, and the term *sakti ḷáfa okhina*, "furrowed bank watercourse," to the Mississippi River. The Choctaw called New Orleans as well as the Lower Mississippi *Bálbancha* or *Málbancha*, a "place of foreign languages," from *bálbaha*, "to talk in a foreign language," and *ásha*, "is there." The Creeks called the Mississippi *wiogufki*, "muddy water," from *wi-*, "water," and *okofki*, "muddy."

MOBILE [moɪˈbiɪl; when attributive, ˈmoɪbiɪl]

1. A city, population 68,202, situated on Mobile River and the head of Mobile Bay. In 1702 Fort Louis de la Mobile, named in honor of Louis XIV, was built by Bienville at what is now called Twenty-seven Mile Bluff on Mobile River; in 1711 the headquarters of the French regime were transferred to the present site of the city of Mobile; in October, 1720, the name of the fort was changed to *Fort Condé de la Mobile* (D'Anville, 1732, has *Fort Condé de la Mobile*); in 1763 Fort Condé was renamed *Fort Charlotte* by the British in honor of the wife of the King of England; on March 14, 1780, fort and town were captured by the Spaniards under Galvez; and in 1813 Mobile surrendered to the American forces under General James Wilkinson. On December 17, 1819, the town of Mobile was reincorporated as a city.

2. A river forty-five miles long, formed by the union of the Alabama and Tombigbee Rivers.

3. A bay receiving the waters of Mobile River.

4. A county established in 1813.

5. Mobile and Bay Shore Junction, a station on the Western Railroad of Alabama in Mobile County.

6. Mobile and Montgomery Junction, a station on the Western Railroad of Alabama in Montgomery County.

7. Mobile Point, the name of a point of land at the entrance of Mobile Bay.[44]

[43] Cuoq, *Lexique de la Langue Algonquine*, page 371, note 2.
[44] See D'Anville's Map, 1732.

The Mobile Indians, who belong to the Choctaw linguistic group, once resided on Mobile River, several miles below the junction of the Alabama and the Tombigbee. They were encountered by early Spanish and French explorers, the tribal name being written in various ways, of which the following are typical:

Mauvila 1540: De la Vega.

Mauilla 1540: Gentleman of Elvas.

Mabila 1540: Ranjel.

Mavila 1544: Biedma.

Mobile 1699: Pénicaut.

Mowill 1758: Du Pratz, II, 213.

The name *Mobile* is probably connected with Choctaw *moeli*, "to row," "to paddle." Hence the noun *moeli* would signify "the rowers."

For the early history of Mobile, see Hamilton, *Colonial Mobile*[2]; and for a detailed account of the Mobile tribe, Swanton, *BAE*, Bul. 73: 150 ff.

MULGA [ˈmʌlgə]

A small town in Jefferson County.

Mulga is said to have been named after an Indian chief. The name may have something to do with Creek *omàlgà*, "all."

MUSCLE SHOALS. See DAGUNAHI, *supra*.

N

NAHEOLA

A small settlement on the west bank of the Tombigbee in the northeastern part of Choctaw County.

The name signifies "white man," from Choctaw *nahollo*.

NANAFALIA [ˌnænəfəˈlaɪə]

A village in Marengo County.

The "hills of Nanafalaya," Romans, 1772; quoted by Hamilton, *Colonial Mobile*[2], p. 282.

Nanafalia P. O. La Tourrette, 1844.

The source of the name is Choctaw *nànih*, "hill," and *falaia*, "long"—"long hill."

NANNA HUBBA [ˌnænə ˈhʌbə]

A bluff just above the junction of the Tombigbee with the Alabama in the southeastern part of Washington County.

Naniaba. Delisle, 1718.

The Naniabas, perhaps a branch of the Choctaw stock, were living at the beginning of the eighteenth century on the bluff which perpetuates this name.

In 1730 they numbered only 50 souls, according to De Lusser, who writes their name *Nanyaba*.[45]

Three different translations of this name have been made: (1) "fish-eaters," from Choctaw *nàni*, "fish," and *àpa*, "eaters"; (2) "fish-killers," from Choctaw *nàni*, "fish," and *àbi*, "killers" —that is, "fishermen"; (3) "hill above," from Choctaw *nànih*, "hill," and *àba*, "above."

I prefer the third translation.

NATCHEZ [ˈnætʃɪz]

A hamlet in Monroe County, recorded in *The Century Atlas*, 1899, but not by Smith, 1891.

The hamlet was probably named after Natchez, Mississippi.

A town of the same name, formerly situated west of the present village of Emauhee in Talladega County, was settled by Natchez Indians shortly after 1730.

Hawkins, *Sketch*, p. 42, spells the name *Nau-chee*, and refers to the present Tallasseehatchee Creek as *Nauchee Creek*, on which the Indians had founded their town.

Natchez Trace is the name that has been given to an old highway running from Nashville, Tennessee, to Natchez, Mississippi.

The origin of *Natchez* is obscure. Gatschet, in what seems to have been his final guess at its meaning, connects the name with Caddo *Na'htcha*, "forest wood," and *da'htcha'hi*, "timber," with which he compares *eda'ktcha*, "forest," in the cognate dialect of *Ta'tassi*. The name, then, may signify "timber land."[46]

NAUFABA CREEK [nɔːˈfɑːbə]

An arm of Chewacla Creek in Lee County. Chewacla, formerly called *Sawacklahatchee*, *infra*, empties into Eufabee Creek in Macon County.

[45] See *Miss. Prov. Archives*, I, 117; cf. also Hamilton, *Colonial Mobile*², pp. 106–107.

[46] See *Louisiana Hist. Quarterly*, XIV, No. 4 (October, 1931), 515.

Naufaba Cr. La Tourrette, 1844.

Naufaba signifies "Beech Creek," from Hitchiti *nofāpi*, "beech tree," a compound of *nofi*, "beech," and *āpi*, "tree." The Creek term for "beech tree" is *nifapi*, which is composed of *nifo*, "beech," and *ápi*, "tree."

NOTASULGA [ˌnoɪtəˈsʌlgə]

A town twelve miles north of Tuskegee in the northern part of Macon County.

Notasulga. Smith, 1891.

The name is probably derived from Creek *noti*, "teeth," and *sulgi*, "many," a term referring perhaps to teeth found at the site of the town.

Notasulga may, however, be a mistake for Creek *nokosálgi*, "bear clan." This analysis, however, I consider very unlikely.

The obscurity of the name is still further heightened by the popularity of the angelica among the Indians as a remedy for various physical ailments.

The Creek term for the angelica (genus *Ammiaceae*) is *notosa;* and a group of plants of this species would be called *notosálgi*, a compound of *notosa* and the collective suffix *álgi*.

NOXUBEE [ˈnaksjŭbiː]

1. A river in Sumter County.

Oka onoxubba or Strong Smelling Water. Purcell Map, *c.* 1770.

2. A station on the Alabama, Tennessee & Northern Railroad in the same county.

Noxubee is the equivalent of Choctaw *nakshobi*, "stinking." *Oka nakshobi*, "stinking water," is often met with in Choctaw.

O

OAKCHIA

A small settlement in the extreme northeast corner of Choctaw County.

Occhoy. Romans, Map, 1772.

Okchai. Adair, pp. 257, 273, 1775.

Hook-choie. Hawkins, *Sketch*, p. 37.

Oke-choy-atte. Schoolcraft, I (1851), 266; *cf.* Gatschet, I, 86.

West Okchai. Smith, 1891.

A Muskogee tribe known as the Okchai, etc., formerly lived near the present *Oakchia*.

The name may be connected with Choctaw *okchāya*, "alive," "living." A Choctaw chief bore the name, apparently similar, of *Oakchia*, or *Oakchiah*[47]—unless his name be intended for Choctaw *okchaha*, "hoed ground," or *oka*, "waters," and *chiya*, "are there"—literally "are sitting there." Compare the Mississippi geographical name *Nusichiya*, "acorns are there."

Though I have suggested several translations, I prefer the one that connects the name with Choctaw *okchāya*.

Halbert and Ball, in *The Creek War*, page 215, record *Okchāya Homma*, "Red Life," or better, "Life Red," as the name of a third lieutenant among Pushmataha's forces in the Creek War of 1813. The second element in this name designates the class to which the warrior belonged.

OAKFUSKEE [oɪkˈfʌskɪ]

1. A creek, tributary to the Tallapoosa, on the boundary between Macon and Montgomery Counties.

Oc-fus-kee. Hawkins, *Sketch*, p. 45.

Oakfuskee or Line C. La Tourrette, 1844.

2. A small settlement in the southern part of Cleburne County.

This name signifies "point between streams," or "promontory," from Creek *ak*, "down in," and *fâski*, "sharp," "pointed."

The original designation of this stream has given way to the present *Line Creek*.

OAKMULGEE [oɪkˈmʌlgɪ]

A creek forming a junction with Little Oakmulgee Creek on the southeastern boundary of Perry County.

A Lower Creek town in Russell County bore this name.

The name signifies "bubbling water," from Hitchiti *oki*, "water," and *mulgi*, "boiling."

OAKTAZAZA

The original Indian name of a creek now called *South Sandy*, in Chambers and Tallapoosa Counties.

Oaktazaza C. La Tourrette, 1844.

The Indian name is composed of Creek *oktahà*, "sand," and

[47] *ASP*, Public Lands, VII (1834), ed. G. & S., pp. 89–91, 135.

sasi, "is there." The element *sasi* is found in several Florida place names—for instance, *Homosassa*, "wild pepper is there," *Wacasassa*, "cattle are there," *Itchepuckesassa*, "tobacco blossoms are there."[48] See *South Sandy Creek*, *infra*.

OCELICHEE [ˌoːsɪˈlaɪtʃɪ]

An affluent of the Chattahoochee River in Chambers County.
O-so li-gee. Early's Map of Georgia, 1818.
Oselichee Cr. La Tourrette, 1833.

Perhaps the source is Creek *àsi*, "cassine" or "yaupon" (*Ilex vomitoria* Ait. or *Ilex cassine* Walt., 1788), and *laichi*, "place," from *laichita*, "to set," "to place." *Àsi* is actually the Creek word for "leaves," those of the yaupon being used in the preparation of the famous black drink of the Southern Indians.

An Upper Creek town was called *Oselanopy*, which is composed of Creek *àsi*, "leaf," *lani*, "yellow," or "green," and *àpi*, "tree."[49]

If the "g" in Early's form *O-so li-gee* indicates a voiced stop, then the second term may be Creek *laiki* or *laigi*, "place," from Creek *laikita*, "to sit."

The postpositive *laiki* or *laigi* is a common element in Creek place names, as, for example, in the Florida names *Tohopekaliga*, "the site of a fort" (*tohopki*+*laiki*), in Osceola County, and *Fumecheliga* (Creek *fàmichà*+*laigi*), "muskmelon place," the designation of a lake near Winter Park. Nevertheless, the modern spelling and pronunciation of the name support the view that the "g" in *O-so-ligee* was sounded like "j" in English "Jim."

OHATCHEE [oːˈhætʃɪ]

1. A creek in Calhoun County, recorded as *Ohatchee C.* by La Tourrette, 1844.

2. A village on the Seaboard Air Line in the same county, recorded by Smith, 1891.

As Ohatchee is just north of another stream called *Tallasseehatchee*, the first element in *Ohatchee* may be Creek *oh* in the sense of "upper," as in Creek *oh-tihe*, "upper room." *Cf.* Creek *oh-hàḷpi*, "outside bark."

The second element is Creek *hàchi*, "stream."

---

48 *Cf.* the writer's *Florida Place-Names of Indian Origin*, pp. 12, 15, 36.
49 Gatschet, I, 128.

OKATUPPA [ˌoːkəˈtʌpə]

1. A creek in Choctaw County.
2. A hamlet in the same county.
Oaktupa (stream). Ludlow, c. 1818.
Oka Tuppah Cr. Smith, 1891.
Choctaw *oktàpi*, "dam" (of water) is the source of this name.
Oktapi is a contraction of Choctaw *oka*, "water," and *tàpa*, "dammed up."

OKETEEOCHENE

A creek entering the Chattahoochee south of Eufaula in Barbour County.
O-ke-teyoc-en-ne. Hawkins, *Sketch*, p. 66. 1799.
Okitiyakni was a Lower Creek town situated about eight miles below Eufaula.
Hitchiti *oki-tiyakni* means "river bend."
The original designation of the creek has been replaced by *Cheneyhatchee*, which probably derives from Creek *àchinà*, "cedar," and *hàchi*, "creek."

OKTAMULKE [ˌɑktəˈmʌlkɪ]

A station on the Louisville & Nashville Railroad in Elmore County.
This name is formed either from Creek *oktaha*, "sand," and *mulki*, "boiling," or from Creek *oktaha* and *omàlkà*, "all"—"Boiling Sand" or "All Sand."
Compare the names *Kymulga* and *Oakmulgee*.

OLUSTEE [oɪˈlʌstɪ]

1. A creek joining Patsaliga Creek in Pike County.
2. A hamlet in Pike County.
This name means "Black Water," from Creek *oi-wa*, "water," and *làsti*, "black." In compound words Creek *oi-wa* is often shortened to *wi*. Cf. *Weolustee, infra*.

OMUSSEE [oɪˈmʌsɪ]

A creek in Henry and Houston Counties.
Omussee C. La Tourrette, 1844.
Omussee is a corruption of the tribal name *Yamassee*, which is derived from Creek *yàmàsi*, "gentle," "quiet."

OPELIKA [ˌoːpɪˈlaɪkə]

A city in Lee County.

When this place was settled, about 1836, it was called *Opelikan*. The name was changed to *Opelika* in 1851.

An Upper Creek town in Coosa County bore this name.

Opelika signifies "big swamp," from Creek *opilwà,* "swamp," and *ḷàko*, "big"—in composition usually *opilḷàko*.

OPINTLOCCO [ˌoːpɪntˈlɑko; ˈpɪntlɑk; ˈpɛntlɑk]

A branch of Chewacla Creek in Macon County.

Opintloco C. La Tourrette, 1844.

This name is a corruption of Creek *opilḷàko*, "big swamp," from *opilwà*, "swamp," and *ḷàko*, "big." *Cf. Swamp Creek, infra.*

OSANIPPA [ˌoːsəˈnɪpə]

1. A creek in Chambers and Lee Counties. A station on the Chattahoochee Valley Railroad in Lee County has taken its name from that of the stream.

Os-sun-nup-pau (Moss Creek): "the bottom rocky with moss." Hawkins, *Sketch*, p. 54.

The source of this name is Creek *Asunàpi*, a compound of *asunwà*, "moss," and *àpi*, "stems." *Hàchi*, "creek," is to be understood.

OSWICHEE [asˈwɪtʃɪ]

A rural community in Russell County.

Oswichee. Smith, 1891.

Oswichee is identical with *Osochi*, the name of an ancient Lower Creek town situated two miles northeast of the present Oswichee.

Swanton, *BAE*, Bul. 73: 165–167, attempts to trace a connection between *Osochi* and a Florida province called in the narratives of De Soto by the names *Uçachile, Uzachil, Veachile,* .and *Ossachile;* but no one seems to have made any effort to translate the name. Perhaps some of the earlier spellings as cited by Hodge, II, 161, may furnish a clue. Here are a few of them:

Oosechee. Adair, p. 257. 1775.

Hooseche. Bartram, p. 462. 1791.

Usechees. Kinnard, in *ASP, Ind. Affairs*, I: 388. 1793.

Oo-se-oo-chee. Hawkins, *Sketch*, pp. 25, 63. 1799.

Oseooche. Wilkinson, in *ASP, Ind. Affairs*, I, 677. 1802.

Among the foregoing spellings the first three seem to point

to Creek *osaichita*, "to drive out"; the last two, however, may possibly contain the Creek diminutive suffix *-uchi* (*-ochi*). Gatschet's forms as given in the *Creek Migration Legend*, I, 142—*Osotchi, Osutchi, Osudshi,* and *Usutchi*—strengthen the view that the name ends in the Creek diminutive.

If the second element of the name signifies "little," the first element may be a corruption of Creek *asi*, "leaf" (of the yaupon); compare the spelling *Oselanopy* (1832) for Creek *asi lani api*, "yellow leaf tree," and *Osceola*, the name of the famous Seminole chief, from Creek *Asi-yahola*, "Black Drink Hallooer." This drink was brewed from yaupon leaves.

The first element also suggests Creek *osa*, "pokeweed" (*Phytolacca americana* L.). The Creeks stained their masks with the juice of the pokeberry.

OTIPALIN. See LOCK, *supra.*

P

PANOLA [pə¹noːlə]

A station on the Alabama, Tennessee & Northern Railroad in Sumter County.

Choctaw *ponola*, "cotton," is the source of this name.

PATSALIGA [ˌpætsə¹laɪgə]

1. A creek that flows through Crenshaw County and unites with the Conecuh in Covington County.

2. Little Patsaliga Creek, a tributary of the Patsaliga in Crenshaw County.

Pad-gee-ligau, from *pad-gee*, a pidgeon [*sic*]; and *ligau*, sit: pidgeon [*sic*] roost. Hawkins, *Sketch*, p. 62.

Pigeon Creek. Early, Map, 1818.

Patsaliga R. La Tourrette, 1844.

An ancient Yuchi village named *Pad-gee-li-gau*, as recorded by Hawkins, *Ga. Hist. Soc. Coll.*, III, 62 ff., was situated at the junction of Padshilaika Creek with Flint River, in Macon County, Georgia. This creek, which is a different stream of course from that bearing the same name in Alabama, is recorded on modern maps of Georgia as *Patsiliga Creek*, a tributary of Flint River, in Taylor County, Georgia.

Patsaliga signifies "Pigeon Roost," from Creek *pachi*, "pigeon," *laiki*, "roost."

Pàchi refers to the passenger pigeon (*Ectopistes migratorius* L.), which has been extinct in the United States since September 1, 1914.

PECKERWOOD CREEK

A tributary of Coosa River in the northwestern end of Coosa County.

Ochoccola Cr. La Tourrette, 1844.

Peckerwood or Ochoccola Cr. Smith, 1891.

The Indian designation of this creek has fallen into disuse.

Ochoccola is a derivative of Creek *wiwa* or *oi-wa*, "water," and *chàkàla*, "woodpecker."

PENNYMOTTLEY [ˌpɛnɪˈmɑtlɪ]

A tributary of Hatchet Creek in Coosa County, east of Coosa River.

Pennymottley Cr. *U. S. Geol. Survey*, Wetumka Quad., Jan., 1903.

This name seems to be corrupted from Creek *pin*, "turkey," and *imaḷa*, "assistant" to a chief. *Imaḷa* is a common element in Creek war names. The Creek voiceless *ḷ*, as in *imaḷa*, is sometimes transcribed with *tl*.

PERMITA

A creek flowing into Big Canoe Creek in St. Clair County. *U. S. Geol. Survey*, Springville Sheet, 1892.

This is an obscure name, and may not be Indian. Note, however, its formal resemblance to Creek *pumita*, "to give us." It might be analyzed, too, as a derivative of Creek *opa*, "owl," *im*, "its," and *ito*, "wood"—"owl wood."

PHENATCHIE [fiːˈnætʃɪ]

A creek in Pickens and Sumter Counties.

The name signifies "squirrels are there," from Choctaw *fàni*, "squirrels," and *asha*, "are there."

An earlier spelling is *Funacha*.

PIL-LOOP. See BIG SWAMP, *supra*.

PINCHONA [pinˈtʃoːnə]

1. A creek joining Pintlalla Creek in Montgomery County.
2. A station on the Louisville & Nashville Railroad in Bald-

win, named by Mrs. J. I. McKinney, wife of a former super-
intendent of this road.

Hawkins, *Sketch*, p. 85, has *Pinchunc*.

The name of the creek is written *Pinchoma* by La Tourrette,
1844, and by Smith, 1891, but *Pinchony* by Rand McNally,
1934.

The first element in *Pinchona* may be Creek *pin(wa)*,
"turkey," and the second is possibly shortened from *chuni-
nitkita*, "to stoop while running." In compounds *pinwa* is generally abbreviated to *pin*.

La Tourrette's form *Pinchoma* may safely be regarded as
erroneous.

PINCHOULEE [pɪnˈtʃuɪlɪ]

A creek tributary to Coosa River from the east in Coosa
County.

Pinchoulee Creek. *U. S. Geol. Survey*, Wetumka Quad., 1903.

This name may mean either "old turkey," from Creek *pin*,
"turkey," and *àchuli*, "old"; or "turkey pine tree," from Creek
pin, "turkey," and *chuli* or *choli*, "pine tree." With the first
translation compare Creek *waka-chuli*, "old bull"; with the
second, Creek *pin-hoti*, "turkey home."

Creek *pinwà*, "turkey," is often shortened to *pin* in compound
words.

Creek *waka*, "cow," is from Spanish *vaca*—as are also Cherokee *waka* and Choctaw *wak*.

PINTHTHLOCKO. See SWAMP CREEK, *infra*.

PINTLALLA [pɪntˈlɑlə]

A creek, tributary to Alabama River, on the northeastern
boundary line of Lowndes County.

Tatum, in 1814, calls this stream *Path-lau-la Creek*. *Pub. Ala.
Hist. Soc.*, *Trans.*, II, 137.

Pilth-lau-le. Hawkins, *Sketch*, p. 85.

Pintlala C. La Tourrette, 1844.

Creek voiceless *l* is transcribed in various ways—with *hl*, *thl*,
nthl, *ntl*, etc.; but I cannot now recall any word in which Creek
k is represented by *l*. The first element in *Pintlalla* is intended
for Creek *opil*, which is itself an abbreviated form of *opilwà*,

"swamp"; the second is probably Creek *łáło*, "fish." The name, then, means "fish swamp" creek.

But if the second element is merely an unusual corruption of Creek *łáko*, "big," the translation will of course be "Big Swamp" Creek. I doubt seriously, however, whether a name ending in Creek *łáko* would show no *k*-sound in any of its variant forms.

Pintlalla is too far east to be considered of Choctaw origin. To the west is Big Swamp Creek, Tatum's *Pil-loop loc, co* of Creek origin; to the south are *Patsaliga* and *Olustee*, both Creek names; to the north lies Autauga Creek. No Choctaw source can be seriously considered for any of these four names.

PONKABIAH [ˈpɔɪŋkɪbaɪ] or [kɔɪŋkɪbaɪ]

An affluent of the Sucarnochee in Sumter County.
Ponkabiah. Smith, 1891.

The source of this name is Choctaw *payki*, "grapes," and *abeha*, "are therein."

The grapes referred to here are probably muscadines or southern fox-grapes, the fruit of *Vitis rotundifolia* Michx., which the Choctaw call *suko*, a term surviving as *soco* in the French dialects of Louisiana.

POTHTACHITTO

One of the branches of Tickabum Creek in Choctaw County.
Pothtachitto. Smith, 1891.

This name is apparently derived from Choctaw [*Bok*, "creek"] *pàtha*, "broad," and *chitto*, "big"—big broad creek.

I doubt whether the first element may be regarded as a corruption of Choctaw *bota*, "pulverized," "powdered," a term that would refer to the sandy bottom of the stream.

PUSHMATAHA [ˌpuʃ-, ˌpʊsmætəˈhɔɪ]

1. A village in Choctaw County.
2. A creek in the same county.

Pushmataha, a noted Choctaw chief, served with 2,500 braves under General Andrew Jackson, and was signally honored by burial, in 1824, in the Congressional Cemetery. He was sixty years old.

The Indian's name is possibly made up of Choctaw *apushi*, "sapling," *im*, "for him," and *àlhtaha*, "ready," a term bestowed on the chief in his early youth.

Or the name may be derived from *apushi*, "sapling," and *imalhtaha*, "prepared," "qualified," the latter word indicating the rank to which the Indian belonged. In war titles *Imaltaha* often appears as *Imataha*.

PUSS CUSS [ˈpʊskʌs]

A creek in Choctaw County.

Pooscoo Paäha. Romans, Map, 1772.

Pooscoos Panha. Purcell, Map, *c.* 1770.

The forms given by Romans and Purcell are intended for Choctaw *puskus*, "child," plus *paya*, "crying"—Crying Child Creek.

Q

QUILBY [ˈkwɪlbɪ]

A creek joining Bodka Creek in Sumter County. A Choctaw town of the same name was situated on Quilby Creek.

Koilbah is the spelling in *The American State Papers*, VII (1834), 84, ed. G. & S.

Quilby was corrupted by the Americans from Choctaw *koi*, "panther," *ai*, "there," and *albi*, "killed"—creek where the panther was killed.

S

SAKTI LUSA. See BLACK BLUFF, *supra.*

SALITPA [səˈlɪtpə]

A village in Clarke County.

Salitpa. Smith, 1891.

This name was formed from *Satilpa, infra,* by transposition of the consonants in the second syllable.

SALT CREEK

A stream uniting with Choccolocco Creek at Jenifer in Talladega County.

Oakchinawa C. La Tourrette, 1844.

Salt Cr. Smith, 1891.

The Indian name of this stream was from Creek *okchanwa*, "salt." It is no longer used.

SANTA BOGUE [ˈsæntə ˌboːg]

A tributary of the Tombigbee in the northeastern end of Washington County.

Senator Bogue. Romans, Map, 1772.

Sinta Bogue. Darby, Map, 1816.

Santabogue. Rand McNally, 1934.

Santa Bogue is derived from Choctaw *sinti*, "snake," and *bok*, "creek."

For the word *bok*, compare *Bogue Chitto* and *Bogueloosa*, *supra*.

SATILPA [səˈtɪlpə]

A creek entering the Tombigbee a few miles below Coffeeville in Clarke County.

Satilpa Cr. Smith, 1891.

The beginning of this difficult name seems to point either to Choctaw *isi*, "deer," or to Choctaw *isito*, "pumpkin."

Perhaps the source is Choctaw *isito*, "pumpkin," plus *ilhpa*, "provisions."

Cf. Salitpa, *supra*.

SAUTA [ˈsɔːtə]

Two creeks, tributaries of the Tennessee River—North Sauta in Jackson County, South Sauta in De Kalb County and on part of the boundary between Jackson and De Kalb.

Sauta C. La Tourrette, 1844.

A Cherokee village was situated on North Sauta Creek near its mouth about 1784.

Sauta comes from Cherokee *itsati*, a word of unknown signification.

SAWACKLAHATCHEE

A creek in Lee and the adjoining county of Macon.

Sawokli was a Lower Creek town on the west bank of the Chattahoochee.

Sawacklahatchee signifies "Raccoon Town Creek" from Hitchiti *sawi*, "raccoon," *okli*, "town," "people," and *hàhchi*, "creek."

Compare *Sowhatchee*, the name of a creek in Early County, Georgia, from Hitchiti *sawi* and *hàhchi*, "creek"—Raccoon Creek.

Sawacklahatchee is now called *Chewacla*, *q. v.*, *supra*.

SEA WARRIOR

A creek in the southeastern end of Choctaw County.

The original name was *Isawaya*, from Choctaw *isi*, "deer," plus *waiya*, "crouching"—Crouching Deer Creek.

SEMINOLE ['sɛmɪnoːl]

A village situated on Blackwater River in Baldwin County. Seminole. *Century Atlas*, 1899.

The name *Seminole*, from Creek *siminole*, "separatist," was applied to a Muskhogean tribe of Florida consisting at first chiefly of immigrants from Alabama and southern Georgia.

SEPULGA [si-, sɪ'pʌlgə]

A river uniting with the Conecuh in the northeastern corner of Escambia County.

The Big Suppulgaws, The Little Suppulgaws. Hawkins, *Ga. Hist. Soc. Colls.*, IX, 79, Feb. 10, 1797.

Supalga. Ludlow, *c.* 1818.

If *Sepulga* is of Creek origin, it may be composed of *ási*, "yaupon," *ápi*, "tree," and *álgi*, "grove." A similar compound, as recorded in Sprague's *Florida War*, p. 360, is *cho-a-la-p-ul-ka*, which is undoubtedly the equivalent of Creek *chuli* or *choli*, "pine," *ápi*, "tree," and *álgi*, "grove."

If *Sepulga*, on the other hand, is of Choctaw origin, it may be a corruption of *shoboli* or *shobulli*, "smoky."

Compare Sobola or Sabougla, a creek in Calhoun County, Mississippi, and Sabougla, a village in the same county, the names of which are derived from Choctaw *shobulli*, "smoky."

I am decidedly of the opinion that *Sepulga* is Creek rather than Choctaw.

SEYOYAH

A creek in Choctaw County.

Seyoyah may be intended for *Sequoya*, the name of the inventor, in 1821, of the Cherokee alphabet, or for Choctaw *isi*, "deer," and *yaiya*, "crying." "Crying Deer" may be the translation of a Choctaw war name.

Sequoya was also known to the whites as *George Gist*, *Guest*, or *Guess*. *Gist*, with its variants, is of course not an Indian name; it survives in *Guess Creek*, Jackson County.

Sikwayi, the Cherokee source of *Sequoya*, cannot be translated.

SHAWNEE [ʃɔɪ'niː; when attributive, 'ʃɔɪniː]

A hamlet in Wilcox County; the name is of fairly recent application.

Shawnee, the name of an Algonquian tribe, is connected with Algonquian *sawano, shawano,* "south" or "southerner."

SHIRTEE ['ʃɜːtiː]

A tributary of Tallasseehatchee Creek in Talladega County.

Shirtee Cr. La Tourrette, 1833.

Shirtee Cr. *U. S. Geol. Survey,* Gantts Quarry Quad., 1917.

Shirtee seems to be derived from Creek *chati,* "red." *Cf. Chartee, supra.* But *shirtee* may be a corruption of Creek *chàto,* "rock."

Both rocks and red clay are found in this locality.

SHOCCO ['ʃako]

The site of a well-known resort two miles northeast of Talladega.

This is a modern name, locally said to be a derivative of Creek *chuko,* "house," with *ļàko,* "big," understood. The name, however, is no doubt shortened from that of the neighboring Creek *Choccolocco, q. v., supra.*

SHOMO CREEK

A western tributary of Alabama River in the southwestern part of Monroe County.

This stream, according to Brannon, *Arrow Points,* Vol. VIII, No. 3, Mar. 5, 1924, p. 42, was named after Dr. Joseph Shomo, a descendant of a United States Army officer who married a Creek woman, a relative of the Weatherfords.

Shomo is apparently derived from Choctaw *shumo,* "thistle," "thistle down." Compare also Choctaw *iti shumo,* "Spanish moss," from which the name *Shomo* may have been shortened.

SHUMULA [ʃu'mʌlə]

A creek joining Sucarnochee Creek northwest of Livingston in Sumter County.

Shumula. *U. S. Geol. Survey,* Epes Quad., 1929.

This name is a corruption of Choctaw *shumbàla,* "cottonwoods" (*Populus* L.).

SIPSEY [ˈsɪpsɪ]

1. A river in western Alabama, entering the Tombigbee River a few miles west of the village of Ridge in Greene County.

2. A creek in Marion and Monroe Counties, joining the Buttahatchie River in Monroe County, Mississippi.

3. Sipsey Fork, a tributary of the Mulberry Fork of the Warrior River in Walker County.

4. A village on the St. Louis-San Francisco Railroad in Walker County.

Cipsi [a bayou]. De Lusser's Journal, 1730, in *Miss. Provo. Archives*, I (1927), 88.

Sipsey R. La Tourrette, 1844.

Sipsi is the Chickasaw-Choctaw name of the tulip poplar.

For *sipsi*, which is not listed in the *Dictionary of the Choctaw Language* (*BAE*, Bul. 46), see *sip-se*, or "poplar," in James Adair's *History of the American Indians*, p. 291, and Cyrus Byington's *Grammar of the Choctaw Language*, p. 323.

Another Choctaw name for the cottonwood is (*a*)*shumbála*.

The Choctaw of Bayou Lacombe, Louisiana, call the cottonwood *pokpo iti*—that is, "cotton tree," from Choctaw *pokpo*, "cotton," and *iti*, "tree." In their pronunciation iti sounds nearly like French *été*.

SOCAPATOY [ˌsakəpəˈtɔɪ]

1. A small affluent of Hatchet Creek in Coosa County.

2. A village on Socapatoy Creek in the same county.

Succauputtoi. Hawkins, *Ga. Hist. Soc. Colls.*, IX, 170, May 6, 1797.

Sucapatoya C. La Tourrette, 1833.

Socapatoyo, Socapatoy Cr. La Tourrette, 1844.

Sakapatayi, an Upper Creek town, was situated on the creek of the same name.

Socapatoy is said to be a derivative of Creek *sakpatagas*, "I lie inside," the term referring to water lilies, the seeds of which were eaten by the natives.[50] This translation is highly uncertain.

[50] Gatschet, I, 143.

SOFKAHATCHEE CREEK [ˌsɔɪfkəˈhætʃɪ]

A creek joining Coosa River about eight miles below Titus in Elmore County.

Sofkee Hatchee. La Tourrette, 1833.

Safgahatchee. La Tourrette, 1844.

This name is derived from Creek *safki*, "hominy," and *hàchi*, "creek."

The local pronunciation, [ˌhætʃɪˈsɔɪfkə], reverses the order of the two elements in the name.

SOUGAHATCHEE [ˌsɔːgəˈhætʃɪ]

An eastern tributary of the Tallapoosa River, a few miles above Carrville in Tallapoosa County.

Sou-go-hat-che [from *sou-go*, "a cymbal," and *hat-che*, "a creek"]. Hawkins, *Ga. Hist. Soc. Colls.*, p. 49, 1799.

Saugahatchee Cr. Smith, 1891.

In 1799 an Upper Creek village was situated on this creek. The name signifies "Rattle Creek," from Creek *saugu*, "a rattle," plus *hàchi*, "creek."

Rattles were made of gourds and also of turtle shells.[51]

SOUTH SANDY CREEK. See OAKTAZAZA, *supra*.

SOUWILPA [suˈwɪlpə]

1. A creek in the southern part of Choctaw County.

2. A village named after the creek.

Souilpa [creek and village]. Smith, 1891.

The origin of this name is obscure. I suggest that it may be a corruption of Choctaw *shaui*, "raccoons," *ai*, "there," and *àlbi*, "killed"—"the creek where raccoons are killed." Choctaw *bok*, "creek," is to be supplied.

For *àlbi* instead of the more usual *àbi*, "killed," compare the name of a creek in Lauderdale County, Mississippi, *shukhata àlbi bok*, which Halbert translates by "where opossums are killed creek."[52] This name appears as "Chokatalbi Creek" in the *Amer. State Papers*, Pub. Lands, Vol. VII (1834), p. 59, ed. G. & S.

SUCARNOCHEE [ˌsʊkəˈnatʃɪ]

A creek rising in Kemper County, Mississippi, and flowing southeastward into Tombigbee in Sumter County, Alabama.

[51] Swanton, *BAE*, Rep. 42: 521–522.
[52] Pub. of the *Alabama Hist. Soc.*, III, 76.

Sucarnoochee, the spelling given by the United States Geographic Board, is not in accord with the local pronunciation.

Sook hanatcha. Romans, Map, 1772.

Sucarnochee. La Tourrette, 1844.

The source of this name is Choctaw *shukha*, "hog," *in*, "its," and *hàcha*, "river"—Hog River.[53]

The translation "Hog's Backbone," as given in Hamilton's *Colonial Mobile*, p. 281, footnote 1, would connect the name incorrectly with Choctaw *shukha nahchàba*.

SWAMP CREEK

A creek just west of Nixburg in Coosa County.

The original Indian name of this stream is no longer used. It was *Pinththlocko*, according to La Tourrette, 1833 and 1844, a name meaning "big swamp," from Creek *opil ḷàko*, "Big Swamp." See *opintlocco*, *supra*.

SYLACAUGA [ˌsɪləˈkɔɪgə]

A city in the southeastern part of Talladega County.

Suillacouga. La Tourrette, 1844.

The source of this name is Creek *suli*, "buzzards'," and *kagi*, "roost," from *kakità*, "to sit."

T

TACOA

A station on the Louisville & Nashville Railroad in Shelby County.

Tacoa. *Century Atlas*, 1899.

Tacoa, as I am informed by Mr. Peter A. Brannon, was named after a Miss Cozart, whose first name was taken from that of Toccoa, a city in Georgia.

Toccoa signifies "Catawba place," from Cherokee *Atagwa* or *Tagwa*, "Catawba Indian," and *hi*, locative; a geographic name in the old Cherokee territory.

For a sketch of Miss Toccoa Cozart's career, see Thos. M. Owen, in *Transactions of the Ala. Hist. Soc.*, IV, 277, footnote 1.

TAGOUACHA

A bayou in Mobile County.

This name seems to be an early variant (1798) of *Toucha* or Touacha, *infra*.

[53] Halbert, *Pub. of the Alabama Hist. Soc.*, III, 70.

If it is a different name, it may be translated by Choctaw *takon*, "peaches," plus *asha*, "are there."

TALLADEGA [ˌtælǝˈdiːgǝ]

1. A city in Talladega County; named in 1833 after an Upper Creek village which occupied its site.

2. A county, created Dec. 18, 1832.

3. A creek tributary to Coosa River in Talladega County.

4. A mountain range in Clay and Talladega Counties.

5. Talladega Springs, a well-known resort near Talladega.

6. Talladega Springs, a village on the Louisville & Nashville Railroad in the southwestern part of Talladega County.

The source of this name is Creek *tálwa*, town, and *átigi*, border—"Border Town"—a name indicating its location on the boundary between the lands of the Creek Indians and those of the Natchez.

The final syllable -*wa* is regularly lost in Creek compound words, as in *fushàchi*, "bird-stream," *okchànàlgi*, "salt clan," *opiḻḻáko*, "big swamp," *pinhoti*, "turkey home," the first elements being respectively *fuswa*, "bird," *okchànwa*, "salt," *opilwà*, "swamp," and *pinwa*, "turkey."

TALLAHATTA [ˌtælǝˈhætǝ]

1. A creek uniting with Bashi Creek in the northwestern part of Clarke County.

2. Tallahatta Springs, a village situated on Tallahatta Creek.

There is a stream of the same name in Newton and Lauderdale Counties, Mississippi. In 1834 it was known as "Tallahatta, or Silver Creek."

The source of this name is Choctaw *táli*, "metal," "rock," plus *hàta*, "white"—"White Rock," that is, "Silver Creek."

TALLAPOOSA [ˌtælǝˈpuːsǝ]

1. A river uniting with the Coosa to form Alabama River.

2. Little Tallapoosa, a river joining the Tallapoosa in Randolph County.

3. A county established Dec. 18, 1832, and named after the river.

There was an ancient Upper Creek town after which the river was named.

Swanton is probably right in suggesting, *Bul. 73: 286*, Choctaw or Alabama *tàli*, "rock," and *pushi*, "pulverized," as the source of the name. But Gatschet, I, 120, 145, connects the name, though doubtfully, with Creek *talepuḷa*, "stranger." Hodge, II, 677, gives variant spellings of *Tallapoosa*.

TALLASSEE [ˌtæləsɪ]

A town situated on the west bank of the Tallapoosa in Elmore County. The town of East Tallassee is on the opposite bank of the river.

White men came to this locality in the first quarter of the nineteenth century, and one of them by the name of Thomas Barnett called the settlement *Tallassee* after an extinct Indian village.

For the meaning of the name, see *East Tallassee, supra*.

TALLASSEEHATCHEE [ˌtæləsɔˈhætʃɪ]

1. A creek at Jacksonville in Calhoun County.
Tallassee Hatchee Cr. La Tourrette, 1844.
An Upper Creek town was situated near this stream.
2. A creek tributary to Coosa River in Talladega County.
Tallassa hat chee. La Tourrette, 1833.
During the second half of the eighteenth century a remnant of the Natchez tribe resided on this stream; hence *Tallassee Hatchee* was formerly designated as *Natchee Creek* (Melish, 1814). *Natchez, supra*, is of dubious origin.

Tallasseehatchee has been interpreted as "Old Town Creek," from Creek *tàlwa*, "town," *hasi*, "old," and *hàchi*, "creek"; but see *East Tallassee, supra*.

TALLATCHIE [təˈlætʃɪ]

A creek in Monroe County.
The first element is either Choctaw *tala*, "palmetto" (*Serenoa serrulata*) or *tàli*, "rock"; the second is Choctaw *hàcha*, "river," or perhaps *asha*, "are there."
If *asha* is correct, then the first element is plural.

TALLATIKPI [ˌtæləˈtɪkpɪ]

A rocky elevation in Clarke County.
This name signifies "Rock Knob," from Choctaw *tàli*, "rock," and *tikpi*, "knob."

TALLAWAMPA [ˌtælə'wɑmpə]

A creek joining the Tombigbee in the southeastern end of Choctaw County.

Talawamba C. La Tourrette, 1833.

Talawappa C. La Tourrette, 1844.

Tallawampa Cr. Smith, 1891.

Brannon suggests a Choctaw compound meaning "to sing and eat" as the possible source of this name, evidently connecting it with Choctaw *taloa*, "to sing," plus *ampa*, "to eat."[54]

This analysis may be correct; or the name may perhaps be derived from Choctaw *taloa*, "to sing," plus *àbi* or *ambi*, "to kill."

The latter combination is found as a personal name in the form *Taloatubbe*, from *taloa*, "to sing," *t*, "and," plus *àbi*, "to kill"—He who sings and kills.[55] Here the connective *t* is used, though it is often omitted between two verbs, as, for example, in Choctaw *ima àbi*, "to give and kill," and *onàbi*, "to arrive and kill," by the side of *imatàbi* and *onatàbi*. The frequent variation between *àbi* and *tàbi* has led to the analogous intrusion of *t*, "and," in compounds in which the connective is clearly superfluous. Thus one finds such spellings as *wakatubbe*, for *wakàbi*, "butcher," from Choctaw *waka*, "cow," plus *àbi*, "killer";[56] and *Tushkatubbee* for *Tashkaàbi*, "warrior killer."[57]

Hence there has arisen the Choctaw war name, *Tubby* or *Tubbee*, "Killer," in spite of its derivation from *t*, "and," plus *àbi*, "to kill."

A similar analogy could be pointed out for *Chubbee*, "killer," a derivative of Choctaw *cha*, "and," plus *àbi*.

TALLAWASSEE [ˌtælə'wɑsɪ]

A tributary of Alabama River in Lowndes County.

Tallawassee Cr. Smith, 1891.

The source of this name is Creek *tàlwa*, "town," and *hasi*, "old"—"Old Town" Creek.

TALUCAH [tə'luːkə]

A village in the northeastern corner of Morgan County.

I have not been able to obtain any reliable data on this name of modern application.

[54] *Arrow Points*, Vol. XI, No. 1 (July 1, 1925), p. 11.
[55] *ASP*, Public Lands, VII, 84, ed. G. & S.
[56] *ASP*, Public Lands, VII, 109, ed. G. & S.
[57] *Ibid.*, 95.

It may be merely a coinage—a fanciful imitation of *Taluga*, in Florida, or of *Tallulah*, in Georgia, or of *Tallula*, in Mississippi.

There is also a Toluca, near Los Angeles, to say nothing of a Mexican Toluca.

Taluga, or *Talucah*, may be from Creek *Tàlako*, "peas."

Tallulah cannot be translated with certainty, but may be connected with Cherokee *atalulu*, "unfinished," "unsuccessful"; *Tallula*, in Mississippi, means "bell," from Choctaw *tàli*, "metal," and *ula*, "sounding"; *Toluca* is possibly from the tribal name *Talujaa* or *Tilijaes*, unless it be an import from Mexico— see Sanchez, p. 439; and *Toluca*, in Mexico, is connected by Peñafiel, II, 293, 294, with Mexican *Tolocan*, "place of the tribe Toloca," a name containing Mexican *toloa*, "to bow the head."

I must not overlook either *Tulucay* (Rancho), California, which is derived from South Wintun or Patwin *tuluka* or *tulukay*, "red."[58]

TATTILABA

A creek tributary to Jackson Creek in Clarke County.

I am inclined to derive this name from Choctaw *iti hàta*, "whitewood" (*Tilia pubescens* Ait.), *illi*, "dead," and *àba*, "above."

The name would refer, then, to a dead tree on a high point. In this vicinity there is a high knob called *Tallatikpi*, q. v., *supra*.

Tattilaba or *Tuttilaba* is also an alternative designation of Tutalosi Creek in Russell County. See *Tutalosi*, *infra*.

I take the *Tattilaba* of Russell County for a derivative of Creek *ito*, "tree," *tali*, "withered," and *àpi*, "trunk"—Withered Tree Trunk.

TAWASHA

A creek in Baldwin County. This stream is now called *Dolive* after Dominique Dolive, or one of the descendants of this early French settler.

Tawasha is clearly a variant of the tribal name *Tawasa*, for which see *Toucha*, *infra*.

Owen, *History*, II, 1304, gives *Tawasa* as the name of the creek in Baldwin County.

[58] Kroeber, *Calif. Pl.-Names*, p. 63.

TAYLOR'S CREEK

A fork of Santa Bogue Creek in Washington County.

Taylor's Creek was formerly called *Bogue Loosa*, from Choctaw *bok*, "creek," and *lusa*, "black"—Black Creek. Romans, Map, 1772, records it as *Bogue Loosa*.

TECUMSEH [tɪ-, ti'kʌmsɪ]

A village on the Southern Railroad in Cherokee County.

Tecumseh, a noted Shawnee chief, was born in 1768 near the present Springfield, Ohio, and was killed on October 5, 1813, near the present Chatam, Ontario, while fighting as an ally of the British against the American troops under Harrison.

At least eight places in the United States bear the name of this Indian.

Tecumseh is derived from Shawnee *Tikamthi* or *Tecumtha*, "one who springs," the name pointing to membership in the gens of the Great Medicine Panther.

Tecumseh was a visitor among the Southern Indians in 1811.

TENNESSEE ['tɛnɪsiː]

1. A river flowing through the northern counties of Alabama.
2. A great valley watered by this stream.

Tennessee was the name of several ancient Cherokee settlements, two of them being in Tennessee and another in North Carolina.

The meaning of *Tennessee* has not been solved, though the name is found in Cherokee as *Tanasi*.

TENSAW ['tɛnsɔː]

1. A river in Baldwin County.
2. A village in the northern part of the same county.

Hawkins, *Sketch*, p. 23, says that "the settlement of Ta-en-sau borders on the Mobile and Alabama, on the left side."

As early as 1708 Tensas slaves had been brought to Mobile. Some years afterwards the Tensas abandoned their settlement in what is now the parish of St. John the Baptist, Louisiana, and moved to the vicinity of Mobile. See Pénicaut, in Margry, V, 509.

The meaning of *Tensaw* is unknown.

TIBBIE [ˈtɪbɪ]

A small town on the Alabama, Tennessee & Northern Railroad in Washington County.

Tibbie, which is of comparatively recent application, seems to be an echo of a name which designates a creek, a river, and a railroad station in Mississippi.

The Mississippi *Tibbie* or *Tibby* is a shortening of *Okatibbee*, which in turn springs from *Oaktibbehaw R.* (Tanner, 1820). *Oaktibbeha* is now the county name in Mississippi, whereas it has been changed to *Okatibbee* as the name of a creek in the same state. (*Century Atlas*, 1899.)

The Alabama name *Tibbee* seems to be connected with *oktibbeha*, for which several translations have been proposed. Three are given here:

1. "Fighting Water," from Choctaw *oka*, "water," and *itibi*, "fighting," because this stream formed a part of the Choctaw-Chickasaw boundary.

2. "Oka Tebeehaw or Noisy Water"—Romans, Map, 1772.

3. "Blocks of ice therein," from Choctaw *okti*, "ice," and *abeha*, "to be in." As *abeha* is plural, *okti* means "blocks of ice."

In De Lusser's *Journal*, January to March, 1730, *octibia* is rendered by *Eaux Glacées*.[59]

I believe the third translation to be correct.

TICKABUM

A creek in the northeastern part of Choctaw County.

Tuckabunne. La Tourrette, 1844.

Tickabum Cr. Colton, 1855.

The local pronunciation is said to be [ˈtɪkəbʌm] or [ˈtɪkm̩bʌm]

Brannon, in *Arrow Points*, July, 1925, p. 12, suggests that the variant *Tuckabum* is connected with Choctaw *tukafa*, "to fire," which may also signify "fired," or "an explosion."

I can suggest no convincing analysis of this name. Perhaps it is from Choctaw *iti*, "wood," plus *hakbona*, "mouldy"; or, from Choctaw *tikpi*, "knob," or "bend in a stream," plus *buna*, "double"; or even from Choctaw *hatakàbi*, "murderer," "man killer."

[59] *Miss. Prov. Archives*, I (1729–1740), 85.

TICKFAW [ˈtɪkfɔɪ]

A station on the Central of Georgia Railroad, in Russell County; a name of fairly recent application.

Riv. Ticfoha. Lafon, 1806.

This station bears the name of a river which rises in Mississippi and empties into Lake Maurepas, Louisiana.

Perhaps from Choctaw *tiak,* "pine," plus *foha,* "rest," "ease."

TIMMILLICHEE'S FORD

A ford on Bodka Creek in Sumter County.

Timmillichee was a Choctaw sub-chief who lived in one of the Choctaw settlements presided over by Mingo Moshulitubbee.

Timmillichee is slightly corrupted from Choctaw *tàmmalichi,* "He who strikes once with the heel or the hand."

Moshulitubbee became chief of the Northeastern Choctaw district in 1809.

TISHABEE [ˈtɪʃbɪ]

A village in Greene County.

Tishabee. Smith, 1891.

Tradition has it that *Tishabee* was the name of an Indian chief who lived in this neighborhood about 1816. La Tourrette, 1844, does not record this name.

The name is from Choctaw *tishu,* "waiter" or "assistant" (to a chief), and *àbi,* "killer"—"the killer of an assistant chief." The termination *-àbi* is extremely common in Choctaw war names.

For many Choctaw personal names, see *Amer. State Papers,* Public Lands, VII (Washington, 1860), pp. 38 ff., ed. Gales & Seaton.

TOHOPEKA [ˌtoːhəˈpiːkə]

A community situated just south of Horseshoe Bend in the Tallapoosa River.

Tohopeka. Smith, 1891.

Tohopeka is derived from Creek *tohopki,* "fort," the name given by the Creek Indians to their fortification at Horseshoe Bend in the present Tallapoosa County. See *Cholocco Litabixee, supra.*

A similar name is found in Osceola County, Florida—that is, *Tohopekaliga,* in which the second element is Creek *laiki,* "site."

TOLLER BOGUE [ˈtɑləˈboːg]

A creek in Washington County.

A corruption of Choctaw *tala*, "palmetto," and *bok*, "creek."

TOMBIGBEE [tɑmˈbɪgbɪ]

1. A river rising in northeastern Mississippi and uniting with the Alabama about forty-two miles north of the city of Mobile. The united streams form the Mobile River.

2. Little Tombigbee: that part of the Tombigbee which lies above the junction of the Warrior and the Tombigbee.

Tombeckbay River. Romans, Map, 1772.

The name is derived from Choctaw *itombi*, "box," "coffin," and *ikbi*, "makers."

Among the Choctaw there was a class of old men who cleaned the bones of the dead and placed them in boxes. Evidently some members of this class must have lived along the Tombigbee.

To the Choctaw they were known as *na foni aiowa*, from *na foni*, "bones," and *aiowa*, "those who pick up the bones" for burial.

A bone picker of the clan was also called *iksa-nam-boola*, according to Claiborne.[60] This term is from *iksa*, "clan," and *nam boḷi*, "which stores or lays up" (bones).

Early French cartographers are misleading in that they name the Tombigbee after the Mobile tribe: Delisle (1718) has *Sources de la Mobile*, Dumont (1753) *Riv. de la Mobille*, Du Pratz (1757) *Mobille R.*, Lafon (1806) *Riv. de la Mobile*. But D'Anville (1732) calls it *Rivière des Tchicachas*, because it rises in the region formerly occupied by the Chickasaw.

In 1735 De Lusser, acting under Bienville's orders, built Fort Tombecbé near the present village of Epes in Sumter County.

TOOMSUBA [ˈtuːmsʊbə]

A creek forming one of the branches of Alamuchee Creek in Sumter County.

Toomsuba Cr. Smith, 1891.

From Choctaw *tūsubi*, "fish hawk"—*Pandion haliaëtus carolinensis* Gmel.

[60] *Mississippi as a Province*, I, 525.

TOUCHA

A creek in Mobile County.

The Tawasa Indians were called *Toasi* or *Tuasi* by the Spanish chroniclers of the sixteenth century; *Touachas* in 1707 by La Harpe, *Journal*, p. 103, and *Taouachas* (1710) or *Touachas* (1723) in the Pénicaut narrative, Margy, 5: 486, 457.

The Tawasa were driven about 1705 by the Creek and Alabama Indians from the region southwest of the Tallapoosa River, and were granted protection by the French colony in the vicinity of the present city of Mobile.

For the ancient location of the *Taouacha* or *Touachas* in the Mobile region, see the De Crenay map, 1733; and for that of the *Tawasa*, see Swanton, *BAE*, Bul. 73, Plate 2.

If *Toucha* is a corruption of *Touacha*, or *Tawasa*, the name may be cognate with Koasati *tabasa*, "widow," "widower." See Gatschet, I, 89.

Brannon informs me that the local pronunciation of the name of this creek is the same as if it were written *Washer*. See *Tagouacha* and *Tawasha*, *supra*.

TUCKABATCHIE [ˌtʌkəˈbætʃɪ]

A station on the Birmingham & Southeastern Railroad in Elmore County.

Tuckabatchee Bend is a sharp curve in the Tallapoosa River at the mouth of Eufaubee Creek in Macon County.

Tuckabatchi was an Upper Creek town on the west bank of Tallapoosa River, in the present Elmore County, Alabama.

Hawkins, *Sketch*, p. 270, says that the derivation of this name is uncertain; that its ancient name is *Is-po-co-gee*; and that the town is situated on the right bank of the Tallapoosa, opposite the junction of Eufaube, two and a half miles below the falls of the river. *Cf.* Swanton, *BAE*, Bul. 73: 277.

Tukabatchi had another old name besides the one mentioned by Hawkins—*Talua fatcha-sigo*, "incorrect town," "one not sufficiently strict." The Creek elements are *tàlwa*, "town," *fàchi*, "right," "straight," and *sigo*, "not." The element *fàchi* is found, too, in *Litafachi*, *supra*, under *Letohatchee*.

The other old name, *Is-po-cogee*, means "town of survivors," from Creek *isipokok'as*, "I put a wrap, etc., around myself."

TULSE

A station on the Louisville & Nashville Railroad in Shelby County.

Tulse may be a variation of *Tulsa*, the name of a city and county, in Oklahoma, which is perhaps syncopated from Creek *tálwa*, "town," plus *hasi*, "old"—"old town."

TUMKEEHATCHEE [ˌtʌmkɪˈhætʃɪ]

A creek tributary to the Tallapoosa in Elmore County.

Tomgahatchee C. La Tourrette, 1833.

Tumkeehatchee is short for *Wetumkeehatchee*, "sounding water creek," from Creek *wi*, "water," plus *tàmkà*, "sounding," plus *hàchi*, "creek." *Cf. Wetumpka, infra.*

TURKEY CREEK

1. A creek in Choctaw County. See *Fakitchipunta, supra.*

2. A station on the Atlanta, Tennessee & Northern Railroad in Choctaw County. The name was suggested by that of the creek.

A Turkey Creek in the northern part of Baldwin County and another in Marengo and Wilcox Counties lie within territory formerly known to the Choctaw. But Turkey Creek, a station on the Louisville & Nashville Railroad, in Jefferson County, is situated too far to the northeast ever to have had a Choctaw name. Moreover, the name of this station is of recent application.

TUSCAHOMA [ˌtʌskəˈhoːmə]

A settlement on the west bank of the Tombigbee, just north of Wahalak Creek, in Choctaw County.

Tuscahoma. La Tourrette, 1844.

The site of *Tuscahoma* was formerly known to the Choctaw as *Bàchcha Chuka*, "Ridge Houses." Romans, Map, 1772, has *Batcha Chukka*.

Tuscahoma is from Choctaw *tàshka*, "warrior," and *homma*, "red"—Red Warrior.

TUSCALOOSA [ˌtʌskəˈluːsə]

1. A city situated at the falls of Black Warrior River in Tuscaloosa County; incorporated Dec. 13, 1819.

2. A county established Feb. 7, 1818; its name coming from *Tuscaloosa*, the Indian term for a river now known as the

"Warrior" or "Black Warrior." This stream, formed by the confluence of Locust Fork and Mulberry Fork in northern Alabama, flows southwestward and joins the Tombigbee near Demopolis in Greene County. De Crenay's Map, 1733, has *Tascaloussa R.*

On Sunday, Oct. 10, 1540, De Soto entered Athahachi, the village of a Mobile chief named *Tascaluça.*

Tuscaloosa is from Choctaw *táshka,* "warrior," and *lusa,* "black."

Another Choctaw name for the Black Warrior in the eighteenth century was *Apotaka hácha,* "Border River," from *apotaka,* "side," and *hácha,* "river," a term designating this stream as the boundary between the Choctaw and the Creek territory.

The Mitchell map of 1755 records it as *Patagahatche River.*

TUSCUMBIA [tʌsˈkʌmbiə]

A city, the capital of Colbert County.

Tuscumbia. Tanner, 1823.

Tuscumbia is usually translated by "Warrior Killer," as if from Choctaw or Chickasaw *táshka,* "warrior," plus *ábi* or *ambi,* "killer."

It is possible, however, that the name has been shortened either from Choctaw *táshka,* "warrior," and *umbáchi,* "rainmaker," or from Choctaw *táskka umba ikbi,* "warrior rain maker." On the important role of the rainmaker among the Choctaws, see H. B. Cushman, *Hist. Ind. Tribes,* pp. 260 ff.

Tuscumbia was a famous Cherokee chief, whose name is perpetuated in that of the Alabama city.

The original site of *Tuscumbia* was known as early as 1780 by the name of *Oka Kapássa,* "cold water," in the Choctaw and Chickasaw dialects, and was therefore first incorporated as *Ococoposo* in 1820. There is a large spring at Tuscumbia. On June 14, 1821, the name was changed to "Big Spring"; in 1822 this name became in turn *Tuscumbia Creek.*

The fact that *Oka Kapássa* is a Chickasaw term points to Chickasaw occupancy of the site of Tuscumbia before the coming of the Cherokee. Both Cherokee and Chickasaw claimed that part of Colbert County lying east of Big Bear Creek. But Colbert County was named for two Cherokee brothers, George and Levi Colbert.

The Cherokee had four settlements in Colbert County during the last quarter of the eighteenth century: (1) Doublehead's village, near George Colbert's Ferry; (2) *Oka Kapàssa*, "Cold Water," a name given to the big spring at Tuscumbia; (3) a small settlement at Muscle Shoals; (4) a large settlement at the mouth of Town Creek.

TUSKEGEE [tʌsˈkiːgɪ]

1. A town in Macon County.
2. Tuskegee Institute in Macon County.

Hawkins, *Sketch*, p. 37, places the town of Tuskegee in the forks of the Coosa and Tallapoosa, where formerly stood the French fort Toulouse.

Tuskegee, the name of a tribe probably of Muskhogean affinity, may be derived from a word signifying "warrior" in several Muskhogean dialects—Alabama *làska*, Choctaw *tàshka*, Creek *taskàya*.

It is possibly a corruption of Creek *tàskiàlgi*, "warriors."

TUSKOONA

A small creek near the northern boundary of Russell County. *Tuskoona* seems to be a corruption of *Tuskena*, or *Tuskenaha*, the name of a chief of the Upper Creeks.

Tuskena may mean "Sapsucker Lieutenant," from Creek *taski*, "sapsucker," and *hiniha*, "lieutenant."

Among the Creeks there was a chief who bore a similar name —*Taski Hajo*, "Mad Sapsucker."

TUTALOSI

A creek in Russell County.

Creek *tutalosi* means "chicken."

Tutalose was a Hitchiti village; but the Hitchiti for chicken is *tatayahi*. Another name for the creek is *Tattillaba* or *Tuttillaba*, *supra*.

TUTTILLABA or TATTILLABA, *supra*.

U

UCHEE

1. A town in Russell County.
2. A creek joining the Chattahoochee in Russell County. One arm of this creek is called *Little Uchee;* another *Big Uchee*.

Uchee or *Yuchi*, the name of an Indian tribe incorporated with the Creek confederacy, probably means "at a distance," from Yuchi *yū*, "at a distance," and *chī*, "sitting down."

For a description of the former Yuchi towns, see Hawkins, *Sketch*, pp. 61 ff.

V

VALLEY CREEK

1. A tributary of the Black Warrior in Jefferson County.

2. A station, named after the creek, on the Louisville & Nashville Railroad in the same county.

This stream is said to have been known to early settlers as "Cuttacochee Creek." On La Tourrette's map of 1844 the name is *Cutocache*.

W. S. Wyman, as quoted by Thomas M. Owen, connects the name with Chickasaw *Okkàttahaka hutche* [hàcha] and translates by "Valley Creek."[61] If this is the source of the name, then the translation should be "hillside stream," from Chickasaw *okkàttahaka*, "hillside," and *hàcha*, "stream," "river"—"valley" in Choctaw-Chickasaw being *okfa* or *kolokbi*.

I am not sure that the original designation of the stream was not "Crosswise (of the valley) Creek," from Chickasaw *okhoatakachi*, "crosswise," with an implied *bok*, "creek," preceding the adjective.

VEAZEY MILL CREEK. *Cf.* CETEAHLUSTEE, *supra.*

W

WACOOCHE [wəˈkuɪtʃɪ]

A tributary of the Chattahoochee in Lee County.

Woc-coo-che (Calf Creek). Hawkins, *Sketch*, p. 54.

Creek *Wakuchi* signifies "calf," being a compound of *waka*, "cow," and -*uchi*, "little."

WAHALAK [ˈwɔɪhɑlɑk; ˈwɔɪhəlɑk]

A tributary of the Tombigbee in Choctaw County.

Wahloh, Wahlok. *ASP*, Pub. Lands, VII (1834), p. 84, ed. G. & S.

Wahalak. Smith, 1891.

[61] Thomas M. Owen, "Valley Creek," Birmingham *Age-Herald* for August 2, 1892, column 1, page 8.

Warloch. Rand McNally, 1834.

Choctaw *Wahhaloha* signifies "pronged"; hence a stream with two branches.

WALLAHATCHEE [ˌwɑləˈhætʃɪ]

A creek tributary to the Tallapoosa River in the southeastern part of Elmore County.

Wallee Hatchee. La Tourrette, 1833.

Wallahatchee. Smith, 1891.

Source: Creek *huḷi* or *hoḷi*, "war," and *àwaḷita*, "to divide," followed by *hàchi*, "creek." In this name the word for "war" must be supplied. The term refers to the privilege of declaring war. There was formerly an Upper Creek town, in the present Tallapoosa County, which bore the name *Huḷi-Waḷi*, "war divider." This town announced the opening of hostilities to its allies.

WATULA [wəˈtuːlə]

1. A creek tributary to the Big Uchee in Russell County.

Watoolee. *U. S. Geol. Survey*, Opelika Quad., 1903–1907.

2. A village in Russell County.

This name has been shortened from Creek *Watula*, "crane," *haki*, "whooping," and *hàchi*, "creek"—Crane-Whooping Creek. Watulahoka was a Lower Creek village near the present Watula.

WAUXAMAKA [ˌwɔːksəˈmeːkə]

A creek in Tallapoosa and Macon Counties, east of East Tallassee.

Wauxamaka Creek. *U. S. Geol. Survey*, Dadeville Quad., 1906.

Wauxamaka is a corruption of the Creek war name *Woksi Miko*. *Woksi* is of unknown signification, though Creek tradition regards it as the name of a Creek clan. *Miko* is Creek for "chief," a substantive.

WAXAHATCHEE [ˌwæksəˈhætʃɪ]

An affluent of the Coosa River on the northeastern boundary of Chilton County.

Waxahatchee Cr. La Tourrette, 1844.

This name is most probably of Creek origin. The first element

may be *woksi*, which occurs as the designation of a Creek clan—
woksálgi—and also as a war name in *Woksi Hadjo* (chief),
Woksi Yahola (hallooer), and similar titles. The exact meaning
of *woksi* is not clear.

The second element of *Waxahatchee*, if the name is Creek, is
hàchi, "stream," "creek"; but *hàchi* may have been substituted
for an earlier Creek *hadjo*.

If *Waxahatchee* is Choctaw, the first element is *waksi*, a highly
opprobious epithet, which Adair, *History of the Amer. Indians*,
p. 199, renders by Choctaw *skoobale*—that is, *isikkopali*,
"cursed." *Cf.* Adair, *ibid.*, p. 143.

The second element, then, would be *hàcha*, "creek." I believe
the name to be Creek rather than Choctaw.

Waxahatchee, whatever its origin may be, certainly has
nothing to do either with Creek *waka*, "cow," or with Choctaw
wak, "cow," neither of which can well be reproduced by *waxa-*.
Among Creek geographic names beginning with *waka* there may
be mentioned the Creek *Wacoochee*, *supra*, as well as the Creek
Wacahoota, "cow barn," and Wacasassa, "cattle range." *Cf.*
the writer's *Florida Place Names of Indian Origin*, pp. 36–37.

Among the Choctaw a few personal names with *wak* are
Wakachàbi or *Wakatàbi*, "butcher," and *Wakhomma*, "red
cow."[62]

Choctaw *wak* and Creek *waka* are loanwords from Spanish
vaca.

WEDOWEE [wi-, wɪˈdauɪ]

1. A fork of Little Tallapoosa River in Randolph County.
2. A village situated on Wedowee Creek.

The village was named about 1834 after an Indian, known
as *Wahdowwee* or *Wahwahnee*, whose village was near the
present Wedowee.

Wahdowwee may be a corruption of Creek *wiwa*, "water,"
and *tawa*, "sumac" (*Rhus* L.), or of Creek *wiwa* and *towi*, "old"
—hence "sumac water," or "old water."

The Indian's other name is obscure. I suggest, however,
Creek *Hoyahàni*, "He who passes by," as a possible source.

Compare *Whoyauni*, the name of a Chiaha chief, which is
derived from the same Creek word.[63]

[62] *ASP*, Public Lands (ed. G. & S.), VII, 58, 83.
[63] Swanton, *BAE*, Rep. 42: 34, and footnote 5.

WEHADKEE [wi-, wɪˈhædkɪ]

1. A creek flowing southward from Randolph County and uniting with the Chattahoochee in Troup County, Georgia.

2. A village in Randolph County.

Wehadkee Cr. Smith, 1891.

This name signifies "white water," the source being Creek *wi*, "water," plus *hàtki*, "white." *Wihàtki* is also the usual term for "ocean."

WELAWNEE [wi-, wɪˈlɔːnɪ]

A creek and rural community in Barbour County.

From Creek *wi*, "water," and *lani*, "yellow."

WELONA [wɪ-, wiˈloːnə]

1. A creek entering Coosa River from the east in the northwestern part of Elmore County.

2. A village near the southwestern boundary of Coosa County.

The location of the creek and of the village is shown on the *U. S. Geol. Survey*, Wetumka Quad., 1903.

The origin of this name is not clear. The first element is probably Creek *wi-*, "water," and the second may be a corruption of Creek *lani*, "yellow"—"Yellow Water" Creek. Or the origin may be sought in Creek *wilana*, Mexican Tea (*Chenopodium ambrosioides* L.), a plant used by the Indians as a remedy for numerous diseases.[64]

WEOGUFKA [ˌwioˈgʌfkə]

1. A creek forming an arm of Hatchet Creek in Coosa County.

2. A village in the same county about 55 miles north of Montgomery.

La Tourrette, 1844, records *Weogufka* as the name of creek and village.

An Upper Creek town was situated on the east bank of Weogufka Creek. Hawkins, *Ga. Hist. Soc. Colls.*, IX, 170, mentions the town of Wiogufki in 1796.

Weogufka is from Creek *wi*, "water," plus *ogufki*, "muddy."

Weogufka, "muddy water," is also Creek Indian for the Mississippi.

64 Cf. Swanton, *BAE*, Rep. 42: 657.

WEOKA [wiᴵoɪkə]

1. A creek tributary to Coosa River in Elmore and Coosa Counties.

2. A hamlet in Elmore County.

"We-wo-cau, from we-wau, water, and wo-cau, barking or roaring."—Hawkins, *Sketch* (1799), p. 40.

Wewoka Cr. Smith, 1891.

Wewoka was an Upper Creek town on a creek of the same name, with forty gun men in 1799.

Hawkins' translation of this name is correct: it is "barking" or "roaring water," from Creek *wi*, "water," plus *wohka*, "barking" or "roaring." On the De Crenay Map, 1733, it is spelled *Ouyoukas*, and placed west of Coosa River.

WEOLUSTEE

A creek in Russell County.

Weolustee Creek. *U. S. Geol. Survey, Seale Quad.*, 1910–1911.

The source of this name is Creek *wi*, "water," and *làsti*, "black"—"Black Water." *Cf. Olustee, supra.*

The name has been corrupted locally to *Will Lester Creek.*

WESOBULGA [ˌwiɪsoᴵbʌlgə]

A creek in Clay County.

Wesobulga Creek. *U. S. Geol. Survey*, Ashland Sheet, 1891.

The source of *Wesobulga* is Creek *wiso*, "sassafras," *àpi*, "tree," and *àlgi*, "grove"—"sassafras tree grove."

This tree (*Sassafras sassafras* L., Karst.) sometimes reaches a height of 125 feet in the Gulf States.

WETUMPKA [wɪ-, wiᴵtʌmpkə]

1. A town on the Coosa River, in Elmore County, twelve miles northeast of Montgomery. Wetumpka was incorporated in 1834.

Little Uchee Creek in Russell County was formerly called *Wetumpka.*

"*We-tum-cau,* from *We-wau,* water, and *tumcau,* rumbling." —Hawkins, *Sketch,* p. 56.

Wetumpka signifies "sounding or tumbling water"—in Creek *wi*, "water," plus *tàmkà*, "sounding."[65]

On the early history of the Upper and the Lower Creek Wetumpka, see Swanton, *BAE*, Bul. 73: 206, 228.

Y

YANTLEY [ˈjæntlɪ]

　　1. A branch of Tickabum Creek in Choctaw County.

　　2. A hamlet in the same county.

Though this looks like an English name, it is certainly a corruption of Choctaw *yanàlli*, "running." *Cf.* Choctaw *oka yanàlli*, "running water."

The name of this creek is recorded as *Yanillo Creek, American State Papers*, Public Lands, VII (1834), 67, ed. G. & S.; and the stream is called *Running Water, ibid.*, p. 73.

D'Anville's *Carte de la Louisiane*, drawn in 1732, records a different stream as *Bouk-oké-yannalé ou Rivière d'Eau Courante*, which is given as a tributary of the *Rivière de la Chasse aux Pascagoulas. Bouk-Oké-Yannalé* is the equivalent of Choctaw *Bok Oka Yanàlli*, "Creek Running Water"—that is, Running Water Creek. The river into which this creek empties bears an Indian name, *Pascagoula*—from Choctaw *pàska*, "bread," and *okla*, "people."

YELLOW LEAF CREEK

　　1. A western tributary of Coosa River in Shelby County.

　　2. A western tributary of the Coosa, in Chilton County.

Oselanopy was the name of an Upper Creek town, probably situated on Yellow Leaf Creek, in Shelby County.

The Creek name was *Asilanapi*, "Yellow Leaf Tree," from *àsi*, "leaf," plus *lani*, "yellow," plus *àpi*, "tree."

Some of the natives still refer to this creek by the Indian name, pronouncing it [ˌaɪsˌnoɪpɪ], according to information given me by Mr. Brannon.

---

[65] *Cf.* Gatschet, I, 150.

BIBLIOGRAPHY

Adair, James. *History of the American Indians* [London, 1775]. Edited
. . . by Samuel Cole Adams, LL.D. Johnson City, Tennessee, 1930.
American State Papers. Indian Affairs, Vol. I. Washington, 1832; Vol.
II. Washington, 1834.
American State Papers. Public Lands, Vol. VII. Published by Gales and
Seaton. Washington, 1860.
Arrow Points. Monthly Bulletin of the Alabama Anthropological So-
ciety. Peter A. Brannon, *editor*. Montgomery, Ala. [various dates].
Bartram, William. *Travels through North and South Carolina, Georgia,
East and West Florida.* . . . Philadelphia, 1791; Reprinted, London,
1792.
Bayo, Ciro. *Vocabulario Criollo-Español Sud-Americano.* Madrid,
1910.
Berney, Saffold. *Handbook of Alabama.* Second and Revised Edition.
Birmingham, Alabama, 1892.
Bourne, E. G., *ed. Narratives of the Career of Hernando de Soto.* Vols.
I–II. New York, 1904.
Brannon, Peter A. "Barbour County Place Names," *Arrow Points,* V,
No. 2 (Aug. 5, 1922), 32–37.
————. "Russell County Place Names," *Arrow Points,* VIII, No. 1
(Jan. 5, 1924), 5–12.
————. "Monroe County Sketches," *Arrow Points,* VII, No. 3
(March 5, 1924), 39–42.
————. "Cochcalechke Creek," *Arrow Points,* IX, No. 5 (Nov. 5,
1924), 67–68.
————. "Certain Place Names in Choctaw County," *Arrow Points,*
XI, No. 1 (July, 1925), 8–12.
————. "Some Peculiarities in Alabama Names," *Arrow Points,* III,
No. 4 (April, 1926), 52–61.
————, *ed. See Arrow Points.*
————. *The Pageant Book.* Montgomery, Alabama, 1926.
Brinton, D. G., *ed. See* Byington.
Bushnell, David I., Jr. "The Choctaw of Bayou Lacomb, St. Tam-
many Parish, Louisiana," *Bureau of American Ethnology,* Bulletin
48, Washington, 1909.
Byington, Cyrus. *Grammar of the Choctaw Language.* Edited by Dr.
[D. G.] Brinton, *Proc. of the Amer. Philosophical Society,* Vol. XI,
No. 84, pp. 317–367. Philadelphia, Feb. 4, 1870.
————. *A Dictionary of the Choctaw Language.* Edited by John R.
Swanton and H. S. Halbert. *Bureau of American Ethnology,* Bulletin
46. Washington, 1915.
Century Atlas of the World. New York, 1899.
Claiborne, J. F. H. *Mississippi as a Province, Territory and State, with
Biographical Notices of Eminent Citizens.* Vol. I. Jackson, Miss.,
1880.
Colton, Geo. W. *Colton's Atlas of the World.* Vol. I, North and South
America. No. 31, *Alabama,* 1855. New York, 1856.

Cuervo, R. J. *Apuntaciones Criticas sobre el Lenguaje Bogotano.* Sexta ed. Paris, 1914.

Cuoq, J. A. *Lexique de la Langue Algonquine.* Montréal, 1886.

Cushman, H. B. *History of the Choctaw, Chickasaw, and Natchez Indians.* Greenville, Texas, 1899.

Dart, Henry P., *ed.* "Note on the Origin of Natchez," *The Louisiana Historical Quarterly,* Vol. 14, No. 4 (Oct., 1931), 575. Baton Rouge, La., 1931.

De Toro, Miguel. *L'Évolution de la Langue Espagnole en Argentine.* Paris [n.d.]

Egli, J. J. *Nomina Geographica.* . . . 2d ed. Leipzig, 1893.

Farris, Tennessee. "Beauty and Humor in Texas Place Names," The Dallas [Texas] *Morning News,* Feature Section, Sunday, November 2, 1930, p. 5.

Feldmann, Jos. *Ortsnamen.* . . . Halle, 1925.

Fifth Report of the United States Geographic Board, 1890 to 1920. Prepared by Charles S. Sloane, Secretary. Washington, 1921.

Gannett, Henry. "The Origin of Certain Place Names in the United States," 2d ed. *United States Geological Survey,* Bulletin 258. Washington, 1905.

Gatschet, Albert S. *A Migration Legend of the Creek Indians.* Vol. I. Philadelphia, 1884: Brinton's *Library of Aboriginal American Literature,* No. 4. Vol. II, St. Louis, 1888: *Trans. Acad. Sci.,* St. Louis, Vol. V, Nos. 1 and 2.

――――. "Towns and Villages of the Creek Confederacy in the XVIII and XIX Centuries," *Pub. of the Alabama Historical Society, Miscellaneous Collections,* I, 386–415. Montgomery, Ala., 1901.

Grossmann, R. "Das Ausländische Sprachgut im Spanischen des Río de la Plata," *Mitteilungen und Abhandlungen aus dem Gebiet der Romanischen Philologie,* Vol. VIII. Hamburg, 1926.

Halbert, H. S., and Ball, T. S. *The Creek War of 1813 and 1814.* Chicago and Montgomery, 1895.

Halbert, H. S. "Creek War Incidents," *Pub. of the Alabama Historical Society, Transactions,* II, 95–119. Tuscaloosa, Ala., 1898.

――――. "Choctaw Indian Names in Alabama and Mississippi," *Pub. of the Alabama Historical Society, Transactions* (1898–1899), III, 64–67. Tuscaloosa, Ala., 1899.

――――. "Funeral Customs of the Choctaws," *Pub. of the Mississippi Historical Society,* III, 353–366. Oxford, Miss., 1900.

――――. "Bernard Romans' Map of 1772," *Pub. of the Mississippi Historical Society,* VI, 415–439. Oxford, Miss., 1900.

――――. "District Divisions of the Choctaw Nation," *Pub. of the Alabama Historical Society, Miscellaneous Collections,* I, 375–385. Montgomery, Ala., 1901.

――――. "The Small Indian Tribes of Mississippi," *Pub. of the Mississippi Historical Society,* V, 302–308. Oxford, Miss., 1902.

――――. "Origin of Mashulaville," *Pub. of the Mississippi Historical Society,* VII, 389–397. Oxford, Miss., 1903.

—————. "Bálbancha, Choctaw Word for the Town of New Orleans," *The Gulf States Historical Magazine*, I, No. 1 (July, 1902), 53–54. Montgomery, Ala., 1903.

—————. "The Year of Tecumseh's Southern Visit," *Pub. of the Alabama Historical Society, Transactions*, IV (1899–1903), 28–29. Montgomery, Ala., 1904.

—————. "The Last Indian Council on Noxubee River," *Pub. of the Mississippi Historical Society*, IV, 271–280. Oxford, Miss., 1907.

—————, ed. *See* Byington.

Hamilton, Peter J. *Colonial Mobile.* . . . Revised and Enlarged Edition. Boston and New York, 1910.

—————, and Owen, Thomas M., *eds.* "Topographical Notes and Observations on the Alabama River, August, 1814. By Major Howell Tatum," *Pub. of Alabama Historical Society, Transactions*, II (1897–1898), 130–177. Tuscaloosa, Ala., 1898.

Handbook of the Alabama Anthropological Society. Compiled by the President [Peter A. Brannon]. Montgomery, Ala., 1920.

Harper, Roland M. "Pronunciation of Certain Place Names," *The Journal of Geography*, Vol. XVI (March, 1918), 255–258. Chicago.

Hawkins, Benj. "A Sketch of the Creek Country in 1798 and 1799," *Georgia Historical Society Collections*, Vol. III. Savannah, Ga., 1848.

—————. "Letters of Benjamin Hawkins, 1796–1806," *Georgia Historical Society Collections*, Vol. IX. Savannah, Ga., 1916.

Hodge, Frederick W., *ed. Handbook of American Indians North of Mexico, Burêau of American Ethnology*, Bulletin 30. Part 1, Washington, 1907; Part 2, Washington, 1910.

Kroeber, A. L. "California Place Names of Indian Origin," *University of California Publications in American Archaeology and Ethnology*, Vol. 12, No. 2, pp. 31–69. Berkeley, June 15, 1916.

La Harpe, Bernard. *Journal Historique de l'Establissement des Français à la Louisiane.* New Orleans, 1831.

Legler, Henry E. "Origin and Meaning of Wisconsin Place-Names, with Special Reference to Indian Nomenclature," *Trans. of the Wisconsin Acad. of Sciences, Arts, and Letters*, Vol. XIV, No. 1 (1903), 16–39. Madison, Wisconsin.

Lenz, R. *Diccionario Etimológico de las Voces Chilenas Derivadas de Lenguas Indíjenas Americanas.* Vols. 1–11. Santiago de Chile, 1910.

Le Page du Pratz, Antoine S. *Histoire de la Louisiane.* Tomes I–III. Paris, 1758.

Lincecum, Dr. Gideon. "Life of Apushimataha," *Pub. of the Mississippi Historical Society*, IX, 415–485. Oxford, Miss., 1906.

Loughridge, R. M., and Hodge, D. M. *Dictionary of the Muskokee or Creek Language in Creek and English.* . . . St. Louis, 1890.

Malone, James. *The Chickasaw Nation.* . . . Louisville, Kentucky, 1922.

Maps: Arrowsmith, 1814; Bellin, 1764; Colton, 1855; D'Anville, 1732; Darby, 1816; De Crenay, 1733; Delisle, 1718; Du Pratz, 1758; Early, 1818; Finley, 1826; Johnson, 1863; La Tourrette, 1833 and 1844;

Ludlow, *c.* 1818; Melish, 1814; Mitchell (John), 1755; Mitchell (S. A.), 1835; Purcell, *c.* 1770; Rand McNally, 1934; Romans, 1772; Smith, 1891; Tanner, 1820 and 1823, etc.

Margry, Pierre. *Découvertes et Établissements des Français dans l'Ouest et dans le Sud de l'Amérique Septentrionale (1614–1754). Mémoires et Documents Originaux.* Tomes I–VI. Paris, 1875–1886.

McKenney, Thomas L., and Hall, James. *History of the Indian Tribes of North America.* Philadelphia and London. Vol. I [n.d.]; Vol. II, Philadelphia, 1842; Vol. III, Philadelphia, 1844.

Middendorf, E. W. *Wörterbuch des Runa Simi oder der Keshua Sprache.* Leipzig, 1890.

Mississippi Provincial Archives. See Rowland and Sanders.

Mooney, James. "Myths of the Cherokee," *Nineteenth Annual Report of the Bureau of American Ethnology,* pt. 1. Washington, 1900.

Nouvelle Biographie Générale. . . . Publiée par Mm. Firmin Didot Frères. . . . 46 vols. Paris, 1852–1866.

Owen, Thos. M. "Valley Creek" . . . , Birmingham *Age-Herald,* August 2, 1892, column 1, page 8. Birmingham, Ala., 1892.

————, ed. "Miss Toccoa Cozart," *Pub. of the Alabama Historical Society, Transactions,* IV (1899–1903), 277, footnote 1. Montgomery, Ala., 1904.

————. *History of Alabama and Dictionary of Alabama Biography.* Vols. I–IV. Chicago, 1921.

Peñafiel, Dr. Antonio. *Nomenclatura Geográfica de México.* Primera Parte, México, 1897; Segunda Parte, México, 1897.

Rand McNally Pocket Maps of Alabama. Chicago, 1934.

Read, William A. "Louisiana Place-Names of Indian Origin," *Louisiana State University Bulletin,* XIX, No. 2. Baton Rouge, La., 1927.

————. "Chas. N. Gould's *Oklahoma Place-Names,*" in *Southwest Review,* Vol. XIX, No. 3 (April, 1934), 346–348. Dallas, Texas, 1934.

————. *Louisiana-French: Louisiana State University Studies,* No. 5. Baton Rouge, La., 1931.

————. *Florida Place-Names . . . : Louisiana State University Studies,* No. XI. Baton Rouge, La., 1934.

Richardson, Warfield C. "Meaning of the Word *Alabama,*" *Pub. of the Alabama Historical Society, Transactions,* IV (1899–1903), 21–22. Montgomery, Ala., 1904.

Romans, Bernard. *A Concise Natural History of East and West Florida.* Vol. 1. New York, 1775.

————. *Map of 1772,* in *Pub. of the Mississippi Historical Society,* VI, 415. Oxford, Miss., 1900.

Rowland, Dunbar, and Sanders, A. G., *eds. and translators. Mississippi Provincial Archives (1729–1740).* French Dominion. Vol. I. Jackson, Miss., 1927.

————. *Mississippi Provincial Archives (1701–1729).* French Dominion. Vol. II. Jackson, Miss., 1929.

————. *Mississippi Provincial Archives* (1704–1743). French Dominion. Vol. III. Jackson, Miss., 1932.

Royce, C. C. "The Cherokee Nation of Indians," *Fifth Annual Report, Bureau of American Ethnology*. Washington, 1887.

Sanchez, Nellie van de Grift. *Spanish and Indian Place-Names of California*. San Francisco, 1914.

Schoolcraft, Henry R. *Historical and Statistical Information, Respecting the History, Condition and Prospects of the Indian Tribes of the United States*. Parts I–VI. Philadelphia, 1851–1857.

Speck, F. G. "The Ethnology of the Yuchi Indians," *Univ. Pa. Anthr. Pub. I, No. I*. Philadelphia, 1909.

Sprague, John T. *The Origin, Progress, and Conclusion of the Seminole War*. New York, 1848.

Street, O. D. "Cherokee Towns and Villages," *Pub. of the Alabama Historical Society, Miscellaneous Collections*, I, 416–421. Montgomery, Ala., 1901.

Swanton, John R. "Indian Tribes of the Lower Mississippi Valley and Adjacent Coast of the Gulf of Mexico," *Bureau of American Ethnology*, Bulletin 43. Washington, 1911.

————. "Early History of the Creek Indians and Their Neighbors," *Bureau of American Ethnology*, Bulletin 73. Washington, 1922.

————. "Social Organization and Social Usages of the Indians of the Creek Confederacy, and Other Papers," *Forty-second Annual Report, Bureau of American Ethnology*. Washington, 1928.

————. "Social and Religious Beliefs and Usages of the Chickasaw Indians," in *Forty-fourth Annual Report, Bureau of American Ethnology*. Washington, 1928.

————. "Source Material for the Social and Ceremonial Life of the Choctaw Indians," *Bureau of American Ethnology*, Bulletin 103. Washington, 1931.

————. Review of William A. Read's "Florida Place-Names . . . ," *American Speech*, Vol. IX, No. 3 (October, 1934), 218–220. New York, 1934.

United States Geological Survey [of Alabama]. Washington, various dates.

United States Official Postal Guide. July, 1925. Washington.

Webster's New International Dictionary of the English Language. Second Edition. Springfield, Mass., 1935.

Wright, Muriel H. "Organization of Counties in the Choctaw and Chickasaw Nations," *Chronicles of Oklahoma*, Vol. VIII (September, 1930), 315–334. Oklahoma City, Okla.

Yelverton, Lois. "Alabama County Seats and Their Early Postal Affairs," *Arrow Points*, III, Nos. 2 and 3 (February–March, 1926), 16–25. Montgomery, Ala.

APPENDIX

1. Names

A

ABESHAI

Obsolete name of a Sumter County stream, probably Kinterbish Creek; said to be from Choctaw *abáchaya*, meaning 'watercourse.'—Foscue, 17.

ALABAMA

"Originally it probably belonged to a single town. The interpretation Professor Read gives is valid, but inasmuch as all of the Southeastern Indians were 'thicket clearers,' I have thought that reference might be had to medicines, the town having been noted for its medicine men or its proximity to quantities of medicine plants. In that case we must suppose *alba* to be understood in an esoteric sense just as the Creek word for 'leaf' [yaupon] came to be applied to the *Ilex vomitoria*"—Swanton, 212. Swanton implies a translation such as 'herb gatherers.'

ALCACHUSKA [ælkə'tʃʌskə]

Obsolete name of Blue Eye Creek, an affluent of the Coosa River in Talladega County. 1823 Tanner map: Alcacuskie; 1833 La Tourette Creek Territory map: Alkachuska. "The second element in the name is Creek *katchki*, 'broken.' The first element may represent Creek *alkaswa*, 'kettles'"—Read, letter to J. B. McM., 30 November 1940.

APALACHEE

"Gatschet was told that the Creeks pronounced this word Apala'chee, with a breathing before the *ch*, and hence argued that it must mean 'people of the other side.' This interpretation has been followed by most writers ever since, but the name is probably from the now extinct Apalachee language which was closer to Choctaw than to Creek and I cannot help thinking that Choctaw *apelachi*, 'helpers,' 'allies,' is more appropriate. The question must be left undecided"—Swanton, 213. Porter's Gap in Talladega County (Upper Creek territory) was formerly known as Apalachee Gap. — Blackford, 56.

ATANCHILUKA

"A creek tributary to Sucarnochee River, in Sec. 14 T. 19 N., R. 3 W., St. Stephens Meridian. From *a*, 'there,' *tāsh*, 'corn,' and *chilluka*, 'shelled' — the creek where corn was shelled" — Read, *AS* 13:79. 1935 Sumter County Soil Map.

B

BIG SHOALS CREEK

Obsolete alternate name of Choccolocco Creek (see p. 18), translation of Creek *choccolocco*. 1838 La Tourette Map; 1878 U.S. Land Office Map of Alabama.

BLACK WARRIOR RIVER

Commonly called The Warrior, although the U.S. Board on Geographic Names ruled in its decision list of 30 June 1941 that Black Warrior is the official name. It is a translation of *tuskaloosa*, q.v., p. 71. 1878 U.S. Land Office Map of Alabama: Tuscaloosa or Black Warrior R. See also Rich, 110–12.

BOGUE [boːg] CREEK

A tributary of the Buttahatchee River in Lamar County. For Choctaw *bok*, 'creek.' The name is thus pleonastic. 1908 Lamar County Soil Map; 1967 Lamar County Highway Map.

BOUGE TUGALOO

Obsolete name of a Sumter County stream, probably the Sucarnochee River, meaning 'creek of the forest people,' from Choctaw *bok* and *iti okla*. — Foscue, 23.

BROKEN ARROW

Read lists Broken Arrow Creek in Russell County, but does not include three other occurrences of the name which are not transferred from Russell County: Broken Arrow Creek in St. Clair County and Broken Arrow Shoals in the Coosa River (1838 La Tourette Map and 1947 USGS Ragland Quadrangle) and Broken Arrow Creek in northwest Tallapoosa County, rising in Clay County (1891 USGS Ashland Sheet and 1909 Tallapoosa County Soil Map). See p. 9 for the origin of Broken Arrow.

BUZZARD'S ROOST

A bluff on the west bank of the Tombigbee River in Sumter County, attested from 1770, translation of Choctaw *sheki a nusi* or *nosi*.—Foscue, 25. See CHICKANOSE, p. 88.

C

CHACTAHATCHE

Early name of the Tombigbee River, possibly a blend of *Chatot*, "the name of a Muskhogean tribe living near Mobile" (Read, p. 19) and Choctaw *hacha*, 'river.'—Rich, 152. Cf. CHOCTAWHATCHEE, p. 19.

CHATTOOGA

"The southern parts of the old Cherokee country were once occupied by tribes of the Creek Confederation and some place names have been taken over from Creek into Cherokee. I suspect that this may be one of them, the first part having reference to 'rocks.' Chato-àlgi would be 'full of rocks,' and the plural ending sometimes drops the *l*"—Swanton, 213.

CHEAHA

The summit of Cheaha Mountain and most of Cheaha State Park are in southwestern Cleburne County; see 1969 USGS Cheaha Mountain Quadrangle. A local "Cheawhaw Town of Indians" is mentioned in Talladega County Deed Records, A:39 (1833). "Contrary to a common opinion, 'the province of Chiaha' visited by De Soto was in Tennessee"—Swanton, 213.

CHELAFAULA [tʃilə'fɔlə] CREEK

Tributary of Chewacla Creek in Lee and Macon counties. 1906 Lee County Soil Map; 1967 Macon County Highway Map. Meaning unknown.

CHEROKEE

"Professor Read has, naturally enough, adopted the old Bureau of Ethnology interpretation, but the application of a Choctaw term to the Cherokee is extremely unlikely. I feel sure that the origin of 'Cherokee' is to be found in Creek *Tciloki* or *Chilokee* which means 'people of a different speech,' though I do not know how the name came to be applied to the historic Cherokee to the exclusion of other non-Creek people. It may have been because they represented a very large invading people from the north who had not been specifically categorized like the tribes nearer the Creeks. Creek *l* would shift to *r* in the Underhill dialect"— Swanton, 213.

CHEWACKLEEHATCHEE [tʃiˌwɑːkləˈhætʃi] CREEK

Variant of CHEWACLA (p. 15) and SAWACKLAHATCHEE (p. 56). 1904 Macon County Soil Map.

CHEWACLA

The railroad station was in Lee County, not Macon. Chewacla Creek rises in Chewacla State Park, south of Auburn. 1894 *Geological Map of Alabama*; 1948 Lee County Highway Map; 1971 USGS Parkers Crossroads Quadrangle.

CHICKANOSE

Now called BUZZARD ROOST BLUFF (q.v., p. 87).—Foscue, 26. Chickanose means 'buzzard's roost' in Choctaw.

CHICKASAW

Obsolete name of a village in Colbert County c1835–1891. Earlier called PORT SMITH and later RIVERTON. 1839 La Tourette Map; 1851–1891 Post Office. In 1825–1837 there was a Chickasaw Indian Agency at or near the site.—Johnson, 285. Named by the Chickasaw Land Co., which operated in the territory occupied by the Chickasaws.—Sandra Sockwell, letter to J. B. McM., 9 September 1983. "While this word [Chickasaw] cannot be translated, it seems probable that the ending is the common Choctaw and Chickasaw locative ending -asha, 'it sits there,' or 'it is there'"—Swanton, 213.

CHIPOLA

"This goes back to a very early period and was probably adopted from Apalachee. As this language was related to Creek, Professor Read's interpretation may, nevertheless, be correct"— Swanton, 213. In addition to the Chipola River listed by Read, there is Chipolo Creek, a tributary of Cheneyhatchee Creek. 1914 Barbour County Soil Map; 1968 USGS Baker Hill Quadrangle.

CHISCA

"The interpretation is correct but the word was often applied to a place occupied by Yuchi Indians. Günter Wagner, a specialist on the Yuchi, informs us that the Root People were an ancient sept or subtribe of these Indians"—Swanton, 213. Chisca is a hamlet (former railroad station) in S33 T3S R14W, and Chisca Dome is a rock formation northwest of the hamlet. 1929 Semmes Map; 1965 Colbert County Highway Map.

E

EASTABOGA

In its *Sixth Report* (1933) the U.S. Geographic Board preferred the spelling Estaboga, which Read accepted (p. 31), but in its Decision List No. 6801 (1968) the U.S. Board on Geographic Names changed the spelling to Eastaboga, conforming with historic local usage. 1848 *Acts of Alabama*, 192; 1892 USGS Springville Sheet; 1972 USGS Eastaboga Quadrangle.

ESCAMBIA

The U.S. Board on Geographic Names ruled in its Decision List No. 1962 (1963) that the Escambia River is formed in Florida by the confluence of Big Escambia Creek (not Big Escambia River) and Little Escambia Creek (not Escambia Creek). The Escambia River is thus not in Alabama, but the two tributary creeks rise in Escambia County, Alabama.

F

FENACHE

Respelling of PHENATCHIE approved by the U.S. Board on Geographic Names 30 June 1937.

FOSHEE

Read derives the name, "of comparatively recent application" from Chickasaw *foshi*, 'bird.' However, in 1941 R. M. Harper, geographer of the Alabama Geological Survey, said that the sawmill village was named for a local family. Stewart J. Foshee (b. 1851) was the owner of several sawmills in Escambia County.—*Memorial Record of Alabama*, 1:965. The pronunciation is ['foːʃi], which supports Harper's derivation.

H

HATCHAOOSE

Obsolete name of the Noxubee River, from Choctaw *hacha*, 'river,' and *usi* or *osi*, 'little.'—Foscue, 36.

HATCHEESOFKA

Variant of SOFKAHATCHEE, q.v., p. 60.

HIGHTOWER (HIGH TOWN) RIVER

Obsolete name of the Coosa River, possibly from Cherokee *itawa*, "itself a name of uncertain origin"—p. xv. Reid, *American Atlas* (1796), Plate 19: High Town R. *American State Papers, Indian Affairs* (1834), 2:153: High Tower R.

HOLETAH

"A creek entering Sucarnochee River near the southern boundary of Sec. 17, T. 19 N., R. 2 W., St. Stephens Meridian [in Sumter County]. From *holihta*, 'fort.'

An ancient Choctaw town, occupying the site of the present De Kalb, in Kemper County, Mississippi, was called *Holita Asha*, 'Fort Place.' Régis du Roullet, writing in 1732, spells the name of the town *Oulitacha*; see *Mississippi Provincial Archives*, I, 154. His translation is correct: 'the fortress is there'"—Read, *AS* 13:79. It is shown on La Tourette's 1839 map and is listed as a current name.—Foscue, 38. 1974 USGS Epes West Quadrangle.

HOLLALLO [hɑ'lɑːlə] LAKE

Evidently an oxbow lake, in northern Sumter County. 1935 Sumter County Soil Map. Listed as LAKE HALLALLA by Foscue (p. 41), who derives the name from Choctaw *halonlàbi*, 'bullfrog,' and cites it on La Tourette's 1839 map. La Tourette 1833 Choctaw Territory map; 1970 USGS Warsaw Quadrangle.

HOMBOGUE

Creek in Sumter County. Interpreted by Foscue (p. 38) as 'red creek.' Another possible interpretation is 'their river,' from Chickasaw *hoo-(i)m-book*.—Munro, 510.

HOTTOCHTACOLLA

Obsolete name of a Greene County stream recorded c1820.—Rich, 291. Origin unknown.

I

IHAGEE

Variant of HIAGGEE (p. 35). 1968 USGS Ft. Benning, Ft. Mitchell, Seale quadrangles.

ISPOCOGEE

Obsolete name mentioned s.v. TUCKABATCHIE, p. 70. "Is-po-cogee is probably not of Creek origin but borrowed from the Shawnee division or tribe known as Kispokotha with which the Tuckabatchie Creeks had intimate relations"—Swanton, 214.

K

KANEE ['kenɪ] CREEK

Tributary of Bodka Creek in Sumter County "said to be of Indian origin but meaning is unknown"—Foscue, 40.

KANETUCHE CREEK

Stream in western Clarke County. Possibly from Choctaw *kantak*, 'smilax.' 1972 USGS Tattlersville and 1978 Winn quadrangles. See KANETUCK, p. 37.

KEEKSABY CREEK

Obsolete Sumter County name "said to be an Indian name but meaning is unknown"—Foscue, 40. Possible derivations are (1) from Choctaw *iksabi*ʔ 'killing Christians' or (2) *iks-aa-bi*ʔ 'where Christians were killed.'—Munro, 511.

KENTUCK

"C. A. Hanna (*The Wilderness Trail*, p. 215) seems to have shown that this was the Iroquois name for the Shawnee town known as Eskippakithiki on the Indian old fields in Clark County, Kentucky, or at least the name of the prairie surrounding it"—Swanton, 213–14. The hamlet Kentuck (Post Office 1872–1902) is referred to in Talladega County Commissioners Court Minutes, B (1853), and the mountain is mentioned in the Talladega *Our Mountain Home*, 28 February 1872, 5/5.

L

LOOKSOOKOLO [ˌlukˈsuːkəlu]

"A creek tributary to the Sucarnochee, in Sec. 22, T. 19 N., R. 3 W., St. Stephens Meridian [Sumter County]. From *luksi*, 'turtle,' *oka*, 'water,' and *hollo*, 'sacred' or 'beloved'—sacred or beloved turtle water"—Read, *AS* 13:79. The name is reported in current use, and is cited from La Tourette's 1839 map, and an alternate explanation is offered: "From Choctaw *lukchuk kaillo* 'tenacious mud'"—Foscue, 43.

M

MIUKA [maɪˈjukə] CREEK

Tributary of the Sukarnochee in Sumter County, from Choctaw *maiyuka*, 'everywhere the same.'—Foscue, 44.

N

NAHEOLA [neˈhiələ]

"Nahollo means literally 'something supernatural,' or 'something remarkable,' and was applied to certain mythic beings before being given to white men. In the present case it would seem impossible to say which was the original source of the name"—Swanton, 214.

NASHOOBA BOGUE

Reported by Rich (p. 402) as probably an early name (c1770) of the Sipsey River or of Trussell's Creek in Greene County. BOGUE is Choctaw *bok*, 'creek.' The Sipsey River is labeled Nashebaw R. on Bernard Romans' map of 1772.

NOOKSABA

"The name appears only on Carey's 1814 map [*Mississippi Territory*]. Seems to be the Noxubee River"—Foscue, 48.

NOTASULGA

"A derivation from the name of the angelica, as indicated in the last paragraph under this head, seems far more probable than the meaning suggested which, however, does give the origin of the plant name itself"—Swanton, 214.

O

OAKACHOY [okə'tʃɔɪ] CREEK

Affluent of Lake Martin (Tallapoosa River) northeast of Nix-burg in Coosa County. 1929 Coosa County Soil Map; 1953 Coosa County Highway Map. Origin unknown.

OAKCHIHOOLA [ˌoːktʃi'huːlə]

Obsolete name of Silver Run [Creek], a tributary of Choc-colocco Creek in Talladega County, reported by Thomas B. Jenkins, grandson of the original settler of the area, in a 1940 interview. "The first element is from *okchai*, the name of an Upper Creek tribe; the second is from Creek *yahola*, the name of the cry uttered at the black drink ceremony"—Read, letter to J. B. McM., 30 November 1940.

OAKLASAUSA [oklə'sɔsə] SANDY CREEK

Tributary of Big Hillabee Creek in northwest Tallapoosa County. 1891 USGS Ashland Sheet. Evidently a variant of OAK-TAZAZA, q.v., p. 47.

OAKOCHAPPA

Obsolete name of Big Bear Creek in Colbert County. Reported from documents of 1795 and 1805 in the Tennessee State Archives by Sandra Sockwell in a letter to J. B. McM., 14 September 1983.

OKEECHEE CREEK

"Probably an early name for Kinterbish Creek. . . . Meaning is unknown"—Foscue, 50. "*Okeechee* may be a form of the verb *ocochchi* 'dip in'"—Munro, 511.

OLAMOYUBEE

"Probably a misspelling of Okanoxubee, one of the early forms of Noxubee"—Foscue, 50. "This name may reflect a Choctaw word or phrase like *okla aa-im-oolabi-ʔ* 'where people were forbidden' or *okla-im-oolabi* 'they forbade him'"—Munro, 511.

OSKIATAPA

Obsolete name of QUILBY CREEK, meaning 'cane cut there.'—Foscue, 50.

OSWICHEE

"If this word, the correct Creek form of which is *O'sochi*, is connected with the Timucua—and I think the evidence for it is rather strong—it would not be interpretable in Creek"—Swanton, 214.

OYPAT OOGOLOO

Obsolete name of a Choctaw region, from Oy-pat-oo-coo-la, 'small nation.'—Foscue, 50.

P

PATAGAHATCHE

Variant of APOTAKA HACHA, 'border river,' cited s.v. TUSCALOOSA, p. 72.

PENOLA

Sometime Sumter County settlement. "Name probably means 'cotton,' from Choctaw *ponola*"—Foscue, 52.

PINTLALLA

"The interpretation given does not seem too plausible. Possibly it is from Creek *pithlo*, 'canoe,' and some form of the verb, 'to pull,' or 'to seize,' which appears in halatäs, 'I pull or seize'"—Swanton, 214.

PONTA ['pɑːntə]

"A creek entering the Sucarnochee in Alabama just east of the southeastern corner of Kemper County, Mississippi. From [Choctaw] *pinti*, 'mouse,' or *panti*, 'cattail'. . . . It is difficult to determine which source is preferable. . . . In the *American State Papers*, *Public Lands*, VII (1834), 56, yet a third, but rare, alternative is introduced for the name of the stream—that is, *Panta Creek*, or *Tasana*. *Tasana* is manifestly intended for Choctaw *Tasannuk*, 'flint'"—Read, *AS* 13:79–80. Foscue (p. 53) accepts the 'cattail' origin. 1974 USGS Tamola and Boyd quadrangles.

Q

QUIBBI

Probably a misspelling of QUILBY [q.v., p. 55].—Foscue, 54.

S

SANUSI [sæn'(h)uːtʃi] CREEK

"A tributary of Looksookolo Creek [in Sumter County]. An arm of Sanusi Creek is called *Little Sanusi*. From [Choctaw] *isanusi*, 'deer lair.' As a verb *anusi* signifies 'to sleep there,' its elements being *a* 'there,'and *nusi*, 'to sleep'"—Read, *AS* 13:80. The spellings SANHOOCHEE and SANNOOSEE are reported in Foscue, 57.

SCOOMA ['skuːmə] CREEK

Tributary of the Noxubee [in Sumter County], "said to be an Indian name but meaning is unknown"—Foscue, 57. "The closest Choctaw word appears to be *(i)skona* 'guts'"—Munro, 511.

SEPULGA

"In the next to last paragraph under this head Professor Read suggests a derivation of the word Sabola or Sabougla, a place in Calhoun County, Miss., from *shobulli*, 'smoky.' However, an old French map dated conjecturally in 1697, has a town or tribe indicated near this point, called Sabougla. Daniel Coxe has this in a corrupted form as 'Samboukia.' I think there is little doubt that it is merely a form of Sawokli and that part of the Sawokli remained in this region until the latter part of the 17th century"—Swanton, 214.

SHOCCO ['ʃɑːko] SPRINGS

Formerly a resort, now a Baptist assembly center, at a cluster of springs three miles northwest of Talladega. Read says (p. 58), "The name . . . is no doubt shortened from that of the neighboring creek *Choccolocco*." When I wrote him that Creek names with initial *ch* were not adopted locally with *sh*, and that there was a Shocco resort in North Carolina popular with Alabamians in the 1850s, he wrote, "You may be right in assuming a transfer of the name from North Carolina to Alabama. . . . The shift from 'ch' to 'sh' would be very unusual unless it took place in a region where French influence formerly prevailed"—Read, in a letter to J. B. McM., 10 November 1944.

SICOLOCCO CREEK

Variant of LOOKSOOKOLO (p. 92). 1974 USGS Emelle and Boyd quadrangles.

SINTA BOGUE CREEK

Tributary of the Tombigbee River in northern Washington County. From Choctaw *sinti*, 'snake,' and *bok*, 'stream.' 1765 British-Choctaw treaty: Cente bonek; 1775 Romans, *Florida*, 329: Sentee Bogua; 1838 La Tourette Map—Owen, 2:1248.

SOCTUM ['sɑːktəm]

A Sumter County settlement on a clay hill is called Soctum Hill. "From Choctaw *sakti humma* 'red bank'"—Foscue, 59. The 1935 Sumter County Soil Map and 1971 USGS Bellamy Quadrangle show also a Soctum Creek, rising near the settlement.

SUCTALOOSA

A Sumter County stream, probably Cotahaga Creek.—Foscue, 61. See BLACK BLUFF, p. 7.

T

TALLADEGA [ˌtælə'dɪgə]

The earliest record of the name is in 1813 in Andrew Jackson, *Correspondence*, 6:355. The Talladega *Sun* on 22 March 1870, 3/2 spelled it Talladigger, which shows the historic and current pronunciation of the stressed syllable, [dɪg], which is often mispronounced by outsiders. The two Talladega Springs listed by Read are one and the same. Talladega "was a border town against the Cherokee and Chickasaw, not the Natchez. The Natchez were late comers into the region and were taken into the Creek Confederacy"—Swanton, 214.

TALLAHALY

"A creek [in Sumter County] tributary to the Tombigbee River. From *tàli*, 'rocks,' and *hieli*, 'standing'—standing rocks creek. Choctaw *hieli* is always plural; its singular is *hikia*"—Read, *AS* 13:80. See U.S. Board on Geographic Names decision list of 30 June 1937 and 1977 USGS Coatopa Quadrangle.

TALLAWYAH

"An affluent of Tallyhaly Creek [in Sumter County]. From *tàli*, 'rocks,' and *waiya*, 'leaning'—leaning rocks creek. The first element can hardly be Choctaw *tala*, 'palmettoes'; yet such an

analysis is not impossible. *Tala* designates the dwarf palmetto"—
Read, *AS* 13:80. 1971 USGS Whitfield Quadrangle.

TASANA. See PONTA, p. 94.

TEN ISLANDS

Shoal in the Coosa River eleven miles east of Ashville, St.
Clair County, site of an Upper Creek village, Otipalin (for *oti*,
'islands' and *palin*, 'ten') and site of Ft. Strother in 1813 (Andrew
Jackson, *Correspondence*, 6:428). See LOCK, p. 42.

TEOC

1. "A creek entering Sucarnochee River in Sec. 20, T. 19 N.,
R. 3 W., St. Stephens Meridian [in Sumter County]. From
[Choctaw] *tiak*, 'pine'"—Read, *AS* 13:80. 1935 Sumter County
Soil Map. 2. Hamlet six miles south of Emelle, spelled TIOC.
1889 U.S. Land Office Map of Alabama.

TIFALLILI

"A tributary of Bodka Creek [in Sumter County]. From
[Choctaw] *iti*, 'tree,' *falaia*, 'tall,' and *illi*, 'dead'—the creek of
the tall dead tree. Here *iti* is singular; for the plural of *falaia*
would be *hofaloha*"—Read, *AS* 13:80. 1935 Sumter County Soil
Map and 1973 USGS Geiger Quadrangle. The stream rises in
Mississippi.

TISHLARKA CREEK

Affluent of the Tombigbee River south of Butler in Choctaw
County. Possibly an Indian name, origin unknown. 1950 Choctaw
County Highway Map; 1978 USGS Butler Quadrangle.

TITI ['taɪtaɪ] BRANCH, SWAMP

1. Stream in eastern Washington County. 1943 USGS Choctaw
Bluff Quadrangle. 2. Swamp in western Baldwin County. 1974
USGS Point Clear and Daphne quadrangles. 3. Swamp in
southern Dallas County. 1957 USGS Carlowville Quadrangle.
The titi is a flowering shrub or tree common in the Gulf states. Its
name may be a Timucuan Indian relic.

TUBBY

"A creek [in Sumter County] tributary to Sucarnochee River.
From [Choctaw] *tàbi*, 'killer,' an extremely popular war name
and termination of war names. Cf. [TALLAWAMPA], page
64"—Read, *AS* 13:80. 1935 Sumter County Soil Map.

TUCKABATCHEE

"From the fact that we find such forms of the name as Totipaches, the first element in this word is probably Creek *tutka*, 'fire,' and the entire name may have had some reference to the prominent part this town played in distributing the busk fire to other settlements"—Swanton, 214.

TUGALOP CREEK

"On Tanner's 1841 map. Perhaps a different form of Bogue Tugaloo"—Foscue, 63.

TUGELO

Obsolete name of a Coosa River affluent draining Howell's Cove in Talladega County, now known as Howell's Branch and Poorhouse Branch. 1832 Talladega County Survey; 1878 U.S. Land Office Map of Alabama. The name, which may have meant 'fork,' originally *dugilu*, "may be a Cherokee borrowing from Chickasaw *tokolo*, 'two'"—Read, letter to J. B. McM., 30 November 1940.

TUSCUMBIA

"The Colbert brothers were Chickasaw, not Cherokee"— Swanton, 215.

U

UCHEE

"The interpretation given may be correct but it is also possible that it has been worn down from Hitchiti Ochesee, 'people of a different speech,' a name also applied to the Lower Creek Indians and to the Ocmulgee river on which they once lived"—Swanton, 215.

V

VOOLA HANATCHA

Obsolete name of a Sumter County stream that "seems to be the modern Sucarnochee River"—Foscue, 63.

W

WAUXAMAKA

"Woksi is the known name of a Creek clan, not merely a traditional name"—Swanton, 215.

WEWOKA

1. A creek, tributary to Tallaseehatchee Creek in Talladega County, rising east of Winterboro; 2. a settlement nearby (Weewokaville Post Office 1838–1875); 3. a spur station (Wewoka Junction) on the L&N Railroad; 4. a spur terminal at a quarry; and 5. the homestead of the pioneer Riser family. Only the stream name and the plantation name are extant. Hawkins (1798–1799 *Sketch*, 40) wrote, "We-wo-kau, from we-kau, water, and wo-cau, barking or roaring." The U.S. Board on Geographic Names, in Decision List No. 6101 (1961) ruled that Weewoka is the official spelling of the creek name, but Wewoka is and historically has been the most common spelling in county and state records, such as the 1832 Talladega County Survey, 1882–1904 Rand McNally railroad maps of Alabama, 1943 USGS Talladega Quadrangle, and 1968 Talladega National Forest Map.

2. Pronunciation

The following list of pronunciations includes (1) some that have apparently changed during the past forty-five years, (2) several local pronunciations that are variants of those reported to Read, and (3) a few that Read did not include. These additions are taken from Foscue's study, from Richard Hartsook's thesis on Alabama place name pronunciation, and from transcriptions I have made of the speech of people familiar with the localities. For the sake of consistency, the symbols are the same as those used by Read.

Autauga [əˈtɔːgə]
Bogueloosa [bogəˈluːsə]
Capshaw [ˈkæpʃɔ]
Channahatchee [tʃɪnɪˈhætʃi]
Cherokee [tʃɛrəˈkiː]
Choccolocco [tʃɑkəˈlɑːkə]
Coosada [kuˈsɑːdə]
Cowikee [kaʊˈægɪ]
Emauhee [ˌiˈmɔi]
Etowah [ˈɛtəwɔ]
Falakto [ˈflæktɔ]
Halawakee [hæləˈwɔkə]
Kewahatchie [ˌkiwɔˈhætʃɪ]
Kowaligi [kaʊəˈlɑɪdʒə]

Ladiga [ləˈdɪgə]
Letohatchee [ˌlitəˈhætʃi]
Naheola [neˈhiələ]
Noxubee [ˈnɑːksjəbɪ]
Patsaliga [pætsəˈlækɪ]
Pushmataha [puʃməˈtɔhɔ]
Salitpa [səˈlɪptə]
Shomo [ʃoːmo]
Sylacauga [ˈsɪləˈkɑːgə]
Tattilaba [ˌtætəˈlebə]
Toomsuba [ˌtumˈsubə]
Uchee [ˈutʃi]
Weogufka [ˌwiəˈgʌfkə]
Wesobulga [ˌwisəˈbʊlgə]

3. Appendix Bibliography

Acts of the General Assembly of the State of Alabama. Montgomery, 1848.
American State Papers. Indian Affairs. Vol. 2, 1834; *Public Lands.* Vol. 7, 1834. Washington: Government Printing Office.
Blackford, Randolph F. *Fascinating Talladega County.* Talladega, Alabama: privately printed, 1957.
Foscue, Virginia O. *The Place Names of Sumter County, Alabama.* Publication of the American Dialect Society No. 65, 1978.
Geological Map of Alabama. University, Alabama: Alabama Geological Survey, 1894, 1926.
Hartsook, Richard. "A Study of the Personal Interview Method for Determining the Locally-Accepted Educated Pronunciation of Alabama Place Names." M.A. Thesis, University of Alabama, 1955.
Highway Maps of Alabama Counties. Montgomery: State Highway Department. Choctaw County, 1950; Colbert County, 1965; Coosa County, 1953; Lamar County, 1967; Lee County, 1948; Macon County, 1967.
Jackson, Andrew. *Correspondence.* Ed. by John S. Bassett. Washington: Carnegie Institution, 1926.
Johnson, Kenneth R. "Highway Markers in Alabama," *Alabama Review*, 36 (October, 1983), 285–86.

La Tourette, John. *An Accurate Map of the State of Alabama*. New York, 1838.

_____. *Map of the Choctaw Territory*. New York: S. Stiles, 1833.

_____. *Map of the Creek Territory*. New York: S. Stiles, 1833.

_____. *Map of Mississippi by Counties, with a Large Portion of Louisiana and Alabama*, 1839.

_____. *Map of the State of Alabama*. Mobile, 1844.

_____. *Map of the State of Alabama and West Florida*. Montgomery, 1856.

Memorial Record of Alabama. 2 vols. Madison, Wisconsin: Brant & Fuller, 1893.

Munro, Pamela. Review of Foscue, *The Place Names of Sumter County, Alabama. Language* 57 (June, 1981), 510–11.

Owen, Thomas M. *History of Alabama and Dictionary of Alabama Biography*. 4 vols. Chicago: S. J. Clarke, 1921.

Rand McNally Co. Maps of Alabama in *Annual Report of the Railroad Commissioners of Alabama*. Montgomery, 1882–1904.

Read, William A. "Ten Alabama Place Names," *American Speech* 13 (February, 1938), 79–80.

Record of Appointment of Postmasters in Alabama 1832–1971. Washington: National Archives Microfilm Publication M841.

Reid, John. "Map of Georgia," *American Atlas*, Plate 19. New York: J. Reid, 1796.

Rich, John S. "The Place Names of Greene and Tuscaloosa Counties, Alabama." Dissertation, University of Alabama, 1979.

Romans, Bernard. "Map of 1772," *Publications of the Mississippi Historical Society* 6 (1900), 415.

Semmes, Douglas R. *Oil and Gas in Alabama*. Alabama Geological Survey, Special Report 15. University, Alabama, 1929. Map by M. M. Valerius Co.

Soil Maps of Alabama Counties. Washington: U.S. Department of Agriculture, Bureau of Soils. Barbour County, 1914; Colbert County, 1965; Coosa County, 1929; Lamar County, 1908; Lee County, 1906; Macon County, 1904; Sumter County, 1935; Tallapoosa County, 1909.

Swanton, John R. Review of Read, *Indian Place Names of Alabama. American Speech* 12 (October, 1937), 212–15.

Talladega [Alabama] *Our Mountain Home*, 28 February 1872.

Talladega [Alabama] *Sun*, 22 March 1870.

Talladega County Commissioners Court Minutes, Vol. B, 1848–1858, n.p.

Talladega County Deed Records, Vol. A, 1833.

Talladega County Survey and Survey Field Notes, 1832.

Talladega National Forest [Map]. Talladega and Shoal Creek District. Washington: U.S. Forest Service, 1940, 1968.

Tanner, H. S. *Map of Georgia and Alabama*. Philadelphia, 1823.

U.S. Board on Geographic Names. Decision Lists. Washington: Department of the Interior, various dates.

U.S. General Land Office. *State of Alabama* [Map]. Washington: General Land Office, 1878, 1889.

U.S. Geographic Board. *Sixth Report 1890 to 1932*. Washington: Government Printing Office, 1933.

USGS Topographic Maps. Washington: U.S. Geological Survey. Ashland Sheet, 1891; Baker Hill Quad., 1968; Bellamy Quad., 1971; Boyd Quad., 1974; Butler Quad., 1978; Carlowville Quad., 1957; Cheaha Mtn. Quad., 1969; Coatopa Quad., 1977; Daphne Quad., 1974; Eastaboga Quad., 1972; Emelle Quad., 1974; Epes West Quad., 1974; Fort Benning Quad., 1968; Fort Mitchell Quad., 1968; Geiger Quad., 1973; Parkers Crossroads Quad., 1971; Ragland Quad., 1947; Point Clear Quad., 1974; Seale Quad., 1968; Springville Sheet, 1892; Talladega Quad., 1943; Tamola Quad., 1974; Tattlersville Quad., 1972; Warsaw Quad., 1970; Whitfield Quad., 1971; Winn Quad., 1978.

INDEX

The Library of Alabama Classics

Quality paperbound editions of the best books on Alabama's history and culture

Up Before Daylight: Life Histories from the Alabama Writers' Project, 1938–1939, James Seay Brown, ed.

90° in the Shade, Clarence E. Cason

Wildflowers of Alabama and Adjoining States, Blanche E. Dean, Amy Mason, and Joab L. Thomas

Horse and Buggy Days on Hatchet Creek, Mitchell B. Garrett

Hugo Black: The Alabama Years, Virginia Van der Veer Hamilton

Seeing Historic Alabama: Fifteen Guided Tours, Virginia Van der Veer Hamilton

A Place of Springs, Viola Goode Liddell

With a Southern Accent, Viola Goode Liddell

Lower Piedmont Country: The Uplands of the Deep South, H. C. Nixon (with a new introduction by Sarah N. Shouse)

Indian Place Names of Alabama, William A. Read (with a new foreword by James B. McMillan)

For a complete listing of Library of Alabama Classics titles write

The University of Alabama Press
University, Alabama 35486–2877